Understanding and Using Theory in Social Work

Understanding and Using Theory in Social Work

JULIETTE OKO

Series Editors: Jonathan Parker and Greta Bradley

LearningMatters

First published in 2008 by Learning Matters Ltd
Reprinted in 2008
Reprinted in 2009

British Library Cataloguing in Publication Data
A CIP record for this book is available from the British Library.

ISBN 978 1 84445 139 5

Cover and text design by Code 5 Design Associates Ltd
Project management by Deer Park Productions, Tavistock
Typeset by PDQ Typesetting Ltd
Printed and bound in Great Britain by Cromwell Press Group, Trowbridge, Wiltshire

Learning Matters Ltd
33 Southernhay East
Exeter EX1 1NX
Tel: 01392 215560
info@learningmatters.co.uk
www.learningmatters.co.uk

Contents

Dedication
To my parents and Evie

Introduction

Understanding and using theory in social work is written for student social workers who are beginning to develop their skills and understanding of the requirements for practice. While it is primarily aimed at students in their first year or level of study, it will be useful for subsequent years depending on how your programme is designed, what you are studying and especially as you move into practice learning. The book will also appeal to people considering a career in social work or social care but not yet studying for a social work degree. It will assist students undertaking a range of social and health care courses in further education. Nurses, occupational therapists and other health and social care professionals will be able to gain an insight into the new requirements demanded of social workers. Experienced and qualified social workers, especially those contributing to practice learning, will also be able to use this book for consultation, teaching, revision and to gain an insight into the expectations raised by the qualifying degree in social work.

Requirements for social work education

Social work education has undergone a major transformation to ensure that qualified social workers are educated to honours degree level and develop knowledge, skills and values which are common and shared. A vision for social work operating in complex human situations has been adopted. This is reflected in the following definition from the International Association of Schools of Social Work and International Federation of Social Workers (2001):

> *The social work profession promotes social change, problem solving in human relationships and the empowerment and liberation of people to enhance well-being.*

> *Utilising theories of human behaviour and social systems, social work intervenes at the points where people interact with their environments. Principles of human rights and social justice are fundamental to social work.*

While there is a great deal packed into this short and pithy definition it encapsulates the notion that social work concerns individual people and wider society. Social workers practise with people who are vulnerable, who are struggling in some way to participate fully in society. Social workers walk that tightrope between the marginalised individual and the social and political environment that may have contributed to their marginalisation.

Social workers need to be highly skilled and knowledgeable to work effectively in this context. In 2002, the then Minister for Health, Jacqui Smith, was keen for social work education and practice to improve. In order to improve the quality of both these aspects of professional social work, it is crucial that you, as a student social worker, develop a rigorous grounding in and understanding of theories and models for social work. Such knowledge helps social workers to know what to do, when to do it and how to do it, while recognising that social work is a complex activity with no absolute 'rights' and 'wrongs' of practice for each situation. We also concur with the Minister in championing the practical focus of social work, of being able to apply our knowledge to help others.

> *Social work is a very practical job. It is about protecting people and changing their lives, not about being able to give a fluent and theoretical explanation of why they got into difficulties in the first place. New degree courses must ensure that theory and research directly informs and supports practice. The Requirements for Social Work Training set out the minimum standards for entry to social work degree courses and for the teaching and assessment that social work students must receive. The new degree will require social workers to demonstrate their practical application of skills and knowledge and their ability to solve problems and provide hope for people relying on social services for support.* (Jacqui Smith, 2002)

The book aims to meet the learning needs outlined in the Department of Health's prescribed curriculum for competence in assessment, planning, intervention and review, incorporating the necessary knowledge, skills and the development of values.

It will also meet subject skills identified in the Quality Assurance Agency academic benchmark criteria for social work. These include understanding the nature of social work and developing problem-solving skills under the following four headings:

- managing problem-solving activities;
- gathering information (including searches and presentation of findings);
- analysis and synthesis;
- intervention and evaluation.

This approach will draw on and rely on you to acquire high-quality communication skills, skills in working with others, and reflective skills in personal and professional development.

The book will also meet the National Occupational Standards (NOS) set for social workers. The Standards state clearly that operational process skills are central to competence. In the language of the NOS social workers must:

- prepare for and work with people and assess their needs and circumstances;
- plan, carry out, review and evaluate in social work;
- support individuals to represent needs, views and circumstances;
- manage risk;
- be accountable with supervision and support for own practice;
- demonstrate professional competence in social work practice.

Book structure

Research indicates that social workers vary considerably in the extent that they make and test hypotheses in practice (Sheppard et al., 2001). A shift towards understanding 'knowledge as process' as opposed to 'knowledge as product' is suggested as one way to integrate theory and practice. These changes to social work education and the implementation of new degree courses mean that there is a need for new, practical learning support material to help you achieve the qualification. *Understanding and using theory in social work* is designed to help you think critically about the knowledge and theory required for understanding social work and apply that understanding to practice situations. The emphasis in this book concerns you achieving the requirements of the curriculum and developing knowledge that will assist you in meeting the Occupational Standards for social work.

The book has five main chapters covering an introduction to understanding social work theory; a consideration of the relationship between theory and practice in social work; the central importance of value and ethics in social work; social work and its organisational context; and a final chapter about putting theory into practice.

Chapter 1 introduces you to what is meant by the term 'theory' and how ideas and knowledge can impact and guide practice. 'Theory' is seen as representing a means of 'making sense' that helps to structure our thoughts and influence our behaviour. Social work is introduced as a 'contested activity' with competing views about its purpose and what social workers do. One way of managing this complexity is the use of an approach known as 'social constructionism' that acknowledges competing meanings. Critical thinking and reflection are therefore integral skills in helping to construct and review your learning or understanding and to inform your practice. These two skills are introduced as dominant themes within this book.

In Chapter 2 we look in more detail at the main ideas, or theories that have shaped social work's development and consider the relationship between theory and practice. Social work is presented as straddling the 'space' between society and the individual or community and therefore it is important to understand social theories about the nature of society, which in turn have influenced explanations about the nature and purpose of social work. We will also look in more detail at some powerful ideas and beliefs that have become established as a dominant discourse around 'rights and responsibilities' and how this has shaped contemporary views about the role of social work.

In Chapter 3, values and ethics are introduced as central in shaping what social workers do and the importance of personal and professional values in shaping the decision-making process. Ethical theories are considered and in particular, virtue ethics are identified as a powerful corrective to the tendency to distance practice outcomes from a consideration of the integrity of the worker and what type of worker we want to be. Such a consideration encourages you to critically review and reflect on your role and the judgements you make and to take seriously the responsibility of your role as a social worker and the practice responsibilities that come with it. Practice matters and questions of values and ethics are always at the heart of what you do.

Chapter 4 explores in more detail the organisational context of social work practice. Since much of contemporary practice still takes place within organisations, the policy context of practice needs to be considered as representing another source of knowledge that also shapes and influences individual practice. You will also consider the role and importance of supervision and the importance of reflective practice in shaping and informing your practice.

In the final chapter, I bring together some of the themes that have been developed in this book and consider how they can be utilised in a practice setting, by considering the use of the 'strengths' perspective (Saleebey, 2006). This provides an example of a practice approach that combines a view about the nature and purpose of social work and stresses the centrality of the worker in its construction, and it therefore provides an example of the how the ideas and themes developed in this book can be demonstrated in a practice context.

Summaries and concluding remarks as well as indicators for further reading are offered at the end of each chapter. You are encouraged to take responsibility for your own learning, identifying your developmental needs and taking your reflections forwards to other texts and other sources of learning to enhance and develop your understanding.

In addition, a glossary of terminology is provided at the end of the book.

Learning features

This book is interactive. You are encouraged to work through the book as an active participant, taking responsibility for your learning, in order to increase your knowledge, understanding and ability to apply this learning to practice. You are encouraged to critically review your understanding of the book as you make your way through each chapter. This is achieved through the use of case studies, research summaries and reflective activities. Together, these are used as aids to help you develop your understanding and provide opportunities for you to reflect and consider how the ideas and knowledge presented can be used to enhance your understanding of the practice of social work. These are learning approaches that encourage 'deep' or meaningful learning, helping you to reflect on your university and practice learning, and should enable you to demonstrate your understanding of the skills and knowledge necessary for effective practice in social work.

Professional development and reflective practice

Great emphasis is placed on developing skills of reflection about, in and on practice. This has developed over many years in social work. It is important also that you reflect prior to practice, if indeed this is your goal. This book will assist you in developing a questioning approach that looks in a critical way at your thoughts, experiences and practice and seeks to heighten your skills in refining your practice as a result of these deliberations. Reflection is central to good social work practice, but only if action results from that reflection.

Reflecting about, in and on your practice is not only important during your education to become a social worker; it is considered key to continued professional development. As we move to a profession that acknowledges lifelong learning as a way of keeping up to date, ensuring that research informs practice and in honing skills and values for practice, it is important to begin the process at the outset of your development. The importance of professional development is clearly shown by its inclusion in the National Occupational Standards and reflected in the General Social Care Council (GSCC) Code of Practice for Employees.

Chapter 1

Introduction to understanding social work theory

A C H I E V I N G   A   S O C I A L   W O R K   D E G R E E

This chapter will begin to help you to meet the following National Occupational Standards.
Key Role 5: Manage and be accountable, with supervision and support, for your own social work practice with your own organisation.
- Manage and be accountable for your own work.
Key Role 6: Demonstrate professional competence in social work practice.
- Work within agreed standards of social work practice and ensure own professional development.

It will also introduce you to the following academic standards as set out in the social work subject benchmark statements.
2.2.1 Defining principles.
Social work is located within different social welfare contexts.
2.2.2 Defining principles.
There are competing views in society at large on the nature of social work and on its place and purpose.
3.1.4 Social work theory.
Research-based concepts and critical explanations from social work theory and other disciplines that contribute to the knowledge base of social work.
3.2.2 Problem-solving skills.
3.2.2.3 Analysis and synthesis.

Introduction

This chapter introduces you to some of the key themes discussed in this book. In particular we will explore different definitions of social work and see that these draw upon different explanations about its nature and purpose. In turn, this leads to the view that social work is a 'contested activity' based on different knowledge sources, ideas and beliefs that we draw upon to help us make sense and which influence our view of what social work is and what we think social work should do. In other words, we begin to see the relationship between thinking and doing, or more specifically, how social work theory can influence our practice, and the importance of recognising the influence of these ideas, knowledge sources and beliefs, through critical thinking and reflection.

By the end of the chapter, you should be able to:

- recognise social work as a contested activity based on different views about its nature and purpose;

- understand the approach known as 'social constructionism' which draws attention to the different ideas or constructions about the nature and purpose of social work as arising from different world views;

- identify what is meant by the term 'theory' and its relationship to informing practice;

- recognise the importance of critical thinking and reflective practice.

Defining social work

To begin with, let us consider definitions about 'what social work is' as in doing so, this helps to reveal the range of 'theories' or ideas and beliefs we draw upon to construct our view.

ACTIVITY 1.1

Write a short paragraph describing what you think social work is about.

Comment

For me, coming up with a satisfactory definition was surprisingly difficult! But I would begin to define social work as:

> *a paid professional activity which involves working with both adults and children to help them try and resolve practical and interpersonal difficulties in order to enable them to function and participate more effectively. This can be on an individual basis or within families, or working with groups or communities to improve their inter-social or personal competencies through the provision of a range of services and interventions. This may also involve the use of statutory controlling powers as well as more therapeutic support.*

In coming up with this definition, I was conscious of how much I wanted to 'pad out' the definition by providing practice examples or to clarify terms such as 'help' or 'enable'. An important consideration therefore, is the context in which social work takes place, which can alter our view of how social work is perceived.

In your definition, you may have described social work as an act of 'helping' directed towards supporting and working with a range of different service users and carers, such as older people or young children or people with learning difficulties, in order to promote their well-being. Such definitions tend to draw upon 'client characteristics' such as age or vulnerability and draw attention to the different 'practice contexts' of social work, seeing that social work takes place in different settings and with a variety of different service users. In addition, the use of the term 'helping' suggests social work is seen as a benign and uncontentious activity, willingly accepted. This was the view adopted by the Department of Health's (2006) recruitment campaign for social work. Here, a social worker is described as:

> *a professional doing a varied and worthwhile job which focuses on improving people's well-being...helping vulnerable people to make crucial decisions to regain control of their lives. They may be parents and children who are struggling in the face of deprivation, disability or abusive behaviour; young adults who are finding it hard to handle the pressures of living independently; people with mental health problems; those with physical or learning disabilities; people with drug or alcohol problems; people suffering from HIV/ AIDS; older people who need support or refugees and homeless people. (p4)*

In contrast, an alternative definition may have emphasised more the types of reasons why social workers are involved in people's lives, such as poverty, ill health, abuse and family breakdown or offending, for instance. These definitions seem to hint more at people's social circumstances or difficulties and may also prompt a consideration of issues of 'social control' and in contrast to the first definition, social work becomes a more contentious activity. This second approach towards defining social work is typified by Jones' (2002) account, which describes social work as:

> *overwhelmingly a class-specific activity... whether the client is old or young, able-bodied or with a special need, an offender, a single parent, an abused child or partner, black or white, clients are most likely to be poor and most likely to be drawn from those sections of the population which enjoy the least status, security and power. (p42, emphasis added)*

A third type of definition may have concentrated more on the skills, tasks or interventions you associate with social work, such as listening, advocacy, assessment, care management or using the law. This is the view adopted by Trevithick (2005), who states:

> *that social work involves working with some of the most complex problems and perplexing areas of human experience and, for this reason, social work is – and has to be – a highly skilled activity... (these) skills and interventions can be used in practice to enhance our effectiveness and help bring about positive outcomes. (p1)*

In highlighting skills and interventions, this definition suggests social work is an applied, interactive activity that draws upon the use of particular knowledge sources and beliefs, and the use of practical and interpersonal skills about how to work effectively with people and problem-solve. Such definitions hint more at the use of values and ethics in social work.

Formal definitions of social work

We can see from the above that trying to define social work can be problematic and points to competing views about its role and purpose. Indeed in their definition, Pierson and Thomas (2002) go on to suggest that social work is an increasingly complex activity. To begin with however, they define social work as *the paid professional activity that aims to assist people in overcoming serious difficulties in their lives by providing care, protection or counselling or through social support, advocacy and community work* (p448). This definition draws heavily on social work's skills and knowledge base. However, later on Pierson and Thomas acknowledge that through its historical development to its present day form social work has come *to be many different things, with large – at times, grandiose – objectives, to an extent that a single summary of what it entail(s) become(s) impossible* (p449).

We can see an example of this grandiose approach in the beginning definition of social work provided by the International Federation of Social Workers (IFSW).

> *The social work profession promotes social change, problem solving in human relationships and the empowerment and liberation of people to enhance well-being. Utilising theories of human behaviour and social systems, social work intervenes at the points where people interact with their environments. Principles of human rights and social justice are fundamental to social work.*
> (IFSW, 2001, www.ifsw.org)

Perhaps what the IFSW definition helps to illustrate most clearly is that social work is a contested activity with competing views about its purpose. In using value terms, such as 'empowerment' and 'liberation', the IFSW is clear the activity of social work should go beyond promoting personal effectiveness, and instead, that social work should promote social change to enhance people's well-being. However, in their definition, the IFSW provide no discussion about how this should be effected and neither is there an acknowledgement of the coercive elements of social work that often elicit both public and political concerns about the role and effectiveness of social work.

Social work as a contested activity

It can be argued that the range and emphasis taken in the different definitions outlined above demonstrate social work to be a contested activity with competing views about its purpose and role. One reason for this, as Parton (1996) argues, is that social work provides an essentially mediating role between the individual and society; it occupies, alongside other welfare professions, the middle 'space' in between. Social work is charged, by virtue of its role and legislative powers to intervene with individuals, groups and communities, to effect some kind of change. It is a socially mandated profession, which within Britain, historically originated from welfare concerns to manage the worst excesses of industrialisation (Parton, 1996). Social work grew out of the slums of developing industrialised cities and has a long association of managing and working with people living and experiencing poverty. However, contemporary social work also deals with people who are vulnerable by virtue of their age or fragility, or mental capacity, or those who are disadvantaged as a result of their social circumstances arising from physical disability or mental ill health; equally there are those who are at risk or are indeed socially excluded due to issues such as lifestyle, drug or alcohol misuse or offending behaviour.

Social work takes place within a variety of different practice settings, which can include for instance, residential homes, hospitals, young offender teams and child protection teams. In addition social work utilises a range of skills and tasks that include practical ones such as problem-solving, administrative tasks and the use of assessment protocols as well as more interpersonal skills such as listening and interviewing. We can add to this a number of intervention methodologies, such as cognitive behavioural therapy or other forms of counselling and brief therapies to effect change as well as drawing on legislative powers in the intervention role.

Social work is a contested activity precisely because of these different factors and also because it mediates between the state and its members. What social workers do and what their responsibilities are will depend significantly on what view is held about the nature of society and the role of the state in welfare. In other words, questions about the nature of society are questions about what kind of society we think we live in or indeed what kind of society we want. This generates questions about what obligations, if any, does society have towards its more vulnerable and disadvantaged members; how do we explain and make sense of issues around social inequality; what rights and responsibilities does society have, and what about individual rights and responsibilities versus collective responsibilities? These are all questions about the type of society or community we live in or would like to see and represent fundamental questions about the type of society we value. These questions generate contested and diverse views about the type of society we live in and invariably impact on views about the nature and purpose of social work. Such views about the purpose and value of social work lie at the heart of considering the issue of what social work is and what it should concern itself with and calls to mind the kinds of 'theories' or knowledge, skills and beliefs which are felt to best guide its activity.

Social work is not a neutral activity and its contested nature reveals itself in terms of changing policy directives, different practice settings and work with different service users, different work patterns between professionals and peers and in our interactions and contact with service users and carers. But it is not just the formal context of 'what social work is' that is contested and changes – our personal views about the nature and purpose of social work do not remain fixed either. Our ideas and beliefs change over time and context as well and are mediated, among other things, by our personal and practice experiences, the development of our professional skills and what we know and learn and our emotions and feelings. These all come together and affect the different ideas and beliefs we have about working with different service users and the range of practice settings that exist and what we consider to be social work. (In developing your understanding of social work as a contested activity, you might wish to broaden your knowledge by following up the reference above to Parton, 1996, or reading other texts, such as Barry, M and Hallett, C (eds) (1998) *Social exclusion and social work*. Both edited texts deal comprehensively with the social challenges that social work is charged with.)

Understanding the role of theory to inform our practice

So far, I have introduced the term 'theory' in inverted commas to refer to the range of knowledge, or ideas, skills and beliefs we draw upon to help us make sense of 'what social work is', which in turn influences our view of 'how to do social work'. In this section I will introduce a definition of what is meant by the term 'theory' and its central importance in helping us inform our view of social work. (These ideas are discussed more fully in Chapter 2 when I look at the distinction between formal and informal theories about the nature of society and how these influence our view about the nature and purpose of social work.)

To begin with however, a theory can be described as representing a set of related ideas and assumptions that are drawn upon to help explain a particular phenomenon. A theory represents therefore an explanatory framework which attempts to help us make sense of the phenomenon in question – in this case, the context of social work. These explanations provide us with an opportunity to hypothesise, or make a judgement, about what we think is going on. In other words, these ideas and assumptions, when acknowledged, provide us with an explanation that can aid our understanding of what the matter is – that is, they help us answer the question of what is going on, what can be done to help and why. Theories essentially help us structure and organise our thinking and are central to helping us make sense of our practice and what we do. In social work, the theories which have predominantly influenced our thinking have been drawn from three main sources, namely; psychological, sociological and biological explanations. These have been drawn upon to help social workers make sense of questions about the nature of social work and its practice context and the difficulties faced by service users and carers.

For instance, we may be working with a mother who is struggling to deal with her nine-year-old son's challenging behaviour. The boy has been diagnosed as having attention deficit hyperactivity disorder (ADHD). In attempting to work effectively with this family, we may draw upon biological explanations to help us understand the diagnosis of ADHD and some of its effects and how it can be managed, e.g. drug therapy. However, we may also draw upon a behavioural explanation in working with the mother to help her deal more effectively, through a behavioural method of intervention, in managing her son's behaviour. Thus by drawing on a range of social work theories we can gain a fuller picture, or explanation of what is going on, but in turn, theories can also redirect us to different ways of thinking and making sense in our work with service users. So, in thinking about our work with this family, we might also draw on attachment theory, as another psychological explanation that could help us in our work, and which seeks to help us understand the relationship between the mother and her son. While it is the assessment process that helps us determine 'what the matter is', it is the explanations, or theories we draw upon, which help us structure and make sense of what the matter is and help guide our interventions with service users. We can see that theories offer explanations, or attempts at making sense, and therefore we can acknowledge that there may be alternative explanations to the same situation. From this view, theories that we draw upon to help us make sense of our social work world may not only be complementary, since they aid and develop our understanding, but theories can also challenge and help us question our initial assumptions and understanding by providing alternative explanations. We can see that social work theories influence and inform our practice, but equally, these theories can also be contested and open to debate. We can extend this idea to questions about the nature or purpose of social work, which reinforce the view that the activity of social work itself is contested and open to debate.

Social constructionism

One way of managing the 'fluidity' of the idea that social work is a contested activity is the adoption of the approach known as social constructionism. This approach sees different ideas or constructions about the nature and purpose of social work as arising from different world views – that is, the bigger picture about what kind of society or community we favour and our view about the role of the state in welfare. Such an approach recognises alternative ways of viewing social phenomena, such as 'social work', since it seeks to describe the alternative ways in which the question 'what is social work?' can be answered. So there are different constructions or meanings about 'what social work is' which are influenced by important factors, such as context, time, legislation and people's behaviour, which influence the judgement that we make. The notion of social constructionism implies therefore that social relations and activities are not universally 'set' or predetermined but instead are open to interpretation and negotiation – in other words, a process of social construction. From this approach, the construction of 'what we know' are products of human meaning-making, not objective fixed facts. Our perception or view about what social work is, therefore, can change according to the practice setting or context we are in and can also change over time due to legislative and policy changes which may influence our view about issues such as responsibility or eligibility for services, for example. Equally, the same issue of concern which can prompt social work intervention can become reinterpreted due to factors such as age or mental capacity or the context in which the behaviour of concern takes place.

Figure 1.1 represents how social work can be viewed from a social constructionist approach. The outer circle represents the role of the state in welfare, with common examples (not a comprehensive list) of different views which can impact and influence its role; for instance, differences in views about eligibility for services, or the use of legislation alter our view about state intervention in welfare. The inner circle represents the role and responsibility of social work and that questions of values and ethics are central to its purpose. This inner circle intersects the outer circle and the different domains which are covered by the role of the state in welfare. However, it is our beliefs about social work and its role and purpose which influence how we see these outer domains and the consequent impact on our practice. Figure 1.1 represents

Figure 1.1 A social constructionist approach toward understanding social work

social work as a contested activity which is constructed and mediated by our values and ethics and the different meanings and emphases we attach to the role of the state in welfare. (Chapter 3 looks in more detail at questions about the role of values and ethics in social work.)

Different discourses of social work

A principal concept in social constructionism is the use of the term 'discourse', which refers to a body of ideas and beliefs which become established as knowledge or an accepted world view. We draw upon these discourses to help us make sense of our social world and, in turn, they frame and influence our understanding.

The term 'discourse' is generally attributed to the French philosopher, Michel Foucault (1926–1984), but as Mills (1997) states, drawing on the work of Macdonnell (1986), *there are a large number of theorists whose work on the theorising of discourse is important* (Macdonnell, 1986, cited in Mills, 1997, p10). A discourse therefore is not just words, either written or spoken, but represents the:

> *grouping of utterances or sentences, statements which are enacted within a social context . . .* determined *by that social context and which contribute to the way that social context continues its existence. Institutions and social context therefore play an important determining role in the development, maintenance and circulation of discourse.* (Mills, 1997, p11; emphasis added)

A discourse therefore has *meaning, force and effect within a social context* (p13) and more often than not, can operate in contrast and in opposition to other discourses, resulting in *practices of exclusion* (p12). So, we can have a discourse around femininity and sexuality, for example, which perpetuates dominant ideas and beliefs about the way women and men should dress and behave and construct their identity, or as I suggest, a discourse around rights and responsibilities. As Mills (1997) concludes, *discourses do not exist in isolation, but are the object and site of struggle...[and]... are thus not fixed but the site of constant contestation of meaning* (p16).

Within the social work literature, discourse analysis has usefully been developed within the work of Fook (2002); Healy (2000, 2005); Parton (2002) and Parton and O'Byrne (2000). Since a discourse has meaning, force and effect, elements of truth, power and knowledge are intrinsic to a discourse. As Parton (2002) states, *Discourses are structures of knowledge claims and practices through which we understand, explain and decide things* (p241). These knowledge claims are given the status of 'truth' by those in power – *we become conscripted into activities that support these 'truths'* (Parton and O'Byrne, 2000, p51). However, from a Foucauldian analysis, 'power' is not just possessed and exercised 'top-down'. Admittedly some knowledge claims acquire the status of 'truth' and hence become powerful; equally, there are alternative knowledge claims which are just as valid, but they remain marginalised or excluded – what Parton and O'Byrne (2000, p52) describe as 'disqualified knowledge'. From this analysis, these alternative discourses can be seen as equally valid and therefore 'truth' becomes a contested concept, open to negotiation and meaning and in turn, 'power' becomes something which we can all exercise. Discourse allows for multiple meaning and acknowledges context and different experiences and interpretation of meaning and validity.

In offering an explanation of our social world, a discourse invariably incorporates its own values which influence our behaviour and the judgements we make. There are three main discourses which I feel have been particularly influential in social work, two of which will be explored in more detail throughout the book. Briefly, however, they include a 'humanist–welfare' discourse, which draws upon assumptions that social and personal problems can best be understood and managed by a focus on rehabilitation and therapy and remains a fundamental belief about the nature of social work. The second viewpoint is discussed more fully in Chapter 2 and is represented by a discourse on 'rights and responsibilities', which draws on assumptions about social and personal rights and responsibilities. The third discourse, discussed more fully in Chapter 5, is what I would describe as an alternative discourse favouring a collective responsibility towards welfare. These different discourses are based on interconnected ideas and beliefs which lead to a particular view or understanding about the nature of social work. For instance, the discourse of 'rights and responsibilities' can emphasise personal or individual rights and responsibilities but undermine a focus on social responsibilities, resulting in an anti-collectivist or minimal role for the state in welfare. Alternatively, an emphasis can be placed more on social rights and responsibilities with a concern for a commitment towards greater social justice for people who are seen as marginalised or socially disadvantaged. This view emphasises the degree to which personal problems are shaped by social structures, and it stresses a collective responsibility for social change in favour of oppressed user groups and is what I describe as the alternative discourse of an empowerment approach.

Different discourses can therefore emphasise particular ideas and beliefs which construct and shape a particular understanding about the role of social work, but the assumptions that lead on from these ideas and beliefs are shaped by the degree of emphasis or focus we place on an idea. Thus we have seen that the degree of emphasis we place on, say, individual rights and responsibilities or social responsibilities leads to competing views about the role and purpose of social work. Equally the discourse around 'what works' includes pragmatic or applied approaches to dealing with social work issues and includes debates about 'evidence-based practice' and 'reflective practice' that can result in different practice outcomes. So the concept of a discourse implies a particular viewpoint, in this case, relating to social work, which is open to different interpretations and meaning-making. Our view about social work becomes constructed therefore through social processes – 'what social work is', is what a particular group or culture or society defines it as. A discourse therefore represents a powerful and fundamental set of ideas and belief which shape our perception of the social phenomena in question – in our case, social work. It legitimates our viewpoint and influences the judgements we make and our behaviour. A discourse seeks to provide an explanation and helps us make sense of what we think of as social work.

I will come back to a discussion about these discourses and examine their impact on the constructions of social work throughout this book. For now, it is important to recognise that the adoption of a particular discourse implies different ways of constructing what social work is and what its role or purpose is.

Critical thinking

An important assumption of the social constructionist approach is that there are alternative ways of making meaning and hence of knowing. The implication of this approach therefore is that we should be critical of ways of knowing as there are always competing ways of understanding and making meaning. Ways of knowing are not always rational. Ideas and beliefs do not always influence our behaviour in the same way or lead to the same outcome, as they will be mediated by our interpretation and the context in which we find ourselves. For example, say in our professional lives we are working in the field of young offenders and our practice is predominantly driven by concerns of reformative or rehabilitative treatment. This is part of a humanist–welfare discourse whereby dealing with offending behaviour is understood as embracing both a social and an individual explanation of crime. However, in our personal lives, if we become a victim of crime, such as burglary or car theft, then we may take an opposing view of offending behaviour where we might focus most strongly on concepts of punishment – in other words, a more punitive approach. This example demonstrates that our perception and understanding of issues can and do vary. We may have a strong emotional response which alters our interpretations of events and thus affects our judgement and behavioural responses. For practical purposes we adopt particular definitions or understandings of social work, but a social constructionist approach cautions against accepting these understandings as unchangeable or indeed, unchallengeable.

Critical thinking thus refers to the process of becoming more aware of the ideas and encompassing beliefs which frame our understanding of social work and their influence on our practice. As Brookfield (1987) states:

> When we become critical thinkers, we develop an awareness of the assumptions under which we, and others, think and act. We learn to pay attention to the context in which our actions and ideas are generated. We become sceptical of quick-fix solutions, of single answers to problems, and of claims to universal truth. We also become open to alternative ways of looking at, and behaving in the world. (pix)

Broookfield (1987) goes onto identify four essential components of critical thinking:

- identifying and challenging assumptions;
- challenging the importance of context;
- imagining and exploring alternatives (which leads to);
- reflective scepticism. (p7–9)

While Brookfield (1987) cautions against claims to 'universal truth', he is not advocating a purely relativist stance. In developing our critical skills,

> we can commit ourselves wholeheartedly to an idea, social structure or cause and still be critically aware. The point is that this commitment is informed; we have arrived at our convictions after a period of questioning, analysis, and reflection. We have examined these ideas, structures, and causes and decided that they are the closest to reality as we understand it...[however]... commitments are made only after a period of critically reflective analysis. (p21)

In their book *Critical thinking for social work*, Brown and Rutter (2006) acknowledge the work of Brookfield (1987) and develop the ideas of Ford et al. (2004, 2005), identifying a critical thinker as one encompassing a number of *requisite intellectual resources* (Brown and Rutter, 2006, pp2–9).

- Background knowledge of the situation in question.
  (In social work, this includes our formal knowledge of social work and our practice experience that helps us develop a depth of knowledge and understanding.)

- Possession of critical concepts.
  (This involves an understanding of the ideas and language associated with critical thinking and argument.)

- Knowledge of critical thinking standards.
  (This involves established standards for appraisal and evaluation of arguments, theory and research and use of judgement.)

- Knowledge of strategies and ways to find things out.
(This involves devising strategies or procedures which help guide our behaviour or thinking.)

- Habits of mind.
(This final point emphasises a value position that a critical thinker also requires certain qualities or 'habits of mind' that enable these intellectual resources to be developed. Given the central importance of values and ethics in informing social work practice, social workers are well placed to develop 'habits of mind' which support and encourage critical thinking.)

Since social work is an applied activity, we cannot separate ideas and beliefs from their influence on our behaviour or practice and this is why we can describe values and ethics as being at the heart of social work practice. Some of these ideas will be taken-for-granted, unquestioned ideas and assumptions which guide and influence our behaviour. Other ideas, however, will be more 'formal', what is traditionally thought of as 'learning' and formally acquired through teaching, reading and practice experience – what is learnt as part of professional education. Equally there are the policies and procedures of an organisation and the legislative framework that increasingly guide contemporary social work practice and the recent introduction of codes of practice for registered practitioners and students.

However, the process of becoming more aware of ideas and their assumptions describes the capacity for critical enquiry and reflection and is a dominant theme in *Understanding and using theory in social work*. We need to be aware of the knowledge, skills and beliefs that inform our practice and which, in this book, are reinforced as a central task of good practice in social work.

Using reflection to inform practice

Critical thinking and reflective practice have been used together to suggest a dynamic process of thinking about and engaging with the ideas and beliefs which inform and influence practice in social work. Indeed the two concepts support each other, as Brechin (2000) suggests. She talks of critical practice in health and social care as *open-minded, reflective appraisal that takes account of different perspectives, experiences and assumptions* (p26). So reflection involves 'thinking about something', be it a concept or idea, feelings or an aspect of our behaviour, using the skills of query and interrogation. We need to ask interrogative questions about the experience in question. Boud et al. (1993, cited in Kuit et al., 2001, p130) suggest that reflection is a generic process which is used to describe the processes involved in exploring experiences in order to enhance our understanding and thus facilitate learning. Reflection is therefore an engaging process that involves asking questions about our practice and its influences, but the process should also be proactive. Being reflective allows us to think critically about the knowledge, skills and beliefs that inform our practice and thus evaluate their impact. It is a way of improving our practice as well as making us aware of 'what worked' and thus identifying examples of good practice. As Kuit et al. (2001) say, it is a means of *questioning why we do something rather than how, and most important of all, learning from this process* (p131). Thus critical thinking is the ability to interrogate the ideas, beliefs and assumptions which we use in our work and recognise alternative views, whereas reflective practice is the process of 'active' engagement with those ideas and alternative views as a means of improving our practice. As social workers we are thus constantly engaged in alternative viewpoints, or even contested views. For many commentators on social work, this is 'the nature of the beast' – social work, in the variety of its settings, deals with uncertainty.

Reflective practice rests on a belief about the nature of social work practice that acknowledges its complexity and uncertainty as a key feature. Reflective practice is part of a *reflective learning paradigm* (Gould, 1996, p1) that attempts to *understand how social workers make judgements and decisions in practice domains which are uncertain and complex*. Gould (1996) suggests that professional knowledge is primarily developed through a practice which is grounded in a systematic analysis of that experience of uncertainty and complexity.

Critical thinking and reflective practice therefore provide us with an important opportunity to think carefully about the knowledge, skills and beliefs which construct and influence our view of social work and to think about how useful these 'theories' are in helping us make sense of our practice. It provides an opportunity to think about what we have learnt and what we do and to make a judgement about the validity of our practice and our learning. Altogether it represents a process which facilitates our learning and understanding by helping us make sense of what we know and how this informs our practice. The following case study provides an example of how a process of critical thinking can be used to consider alternative explanations about our work. Coupled with the use of reflective skills, these can be used to enhance our understanding of the experience and our relationship with service users.

CASE STUDY

Yvette was a newly qualified social worker, who in her placement reports and academic studies was seen as a student with integrity; she was conscientious about her work and in supervision often discussed the complexity of the social work task and how the rhetoric of putting the needs of the service user first could be realised in complex practice situations. On a return course to the university, Yvette talked about the reality of reflective practice. She talked about a recent case she had had where the service user, who was male in his mid-40s, had been released from prison after several years. She talked candidly about what she had learnt from working with service users and the adoption of counselling skills that could usefully facilitate a dialogue between her and the service user. She was confident in her assessment skills and did not feel uncomfortable about working with an ex-offender. However, Yvette soon became frustrated; all her skills were having no effect in her work with the service user; he remained, according to Yvette, reluctant to engage and at times hostile towards her. In turn, Yvette began to feel the same towards him and irritated at his behaviour. She was conscious that she was beginning to label him as 'aggressive and non-compliant'.

CASE STUDY *continued*

Through supervision, which supported a critical and reflective analysis, Yvette began to see things differently. Thinking critically, Yvette realised the process of negative labelling and the hidden assumptions of pathology that were influencing her work. She realised how easily she had fallen into the trap of stereotyping her 'ex-offender'. She then began to think reflectively about her service user's experience of being in prison and what it must have felt like. She imagined the cramped conditions of cell life, and living the majority of time in a cell with another inmate, the lack of privacy, the prevailing culture of bravado and learning to keep your own counsel, and the 'them and us' mentality that existed between the prison officers and the inmates. Yvette began to appreciate the difficult and at times dehumanising experience of prison life and that perhaps her service user's reaction to social work involvement could be better understood from this perspective rather than assuming that the service user was the problem.

Through a process of critical and reflective thought, Yvette tried a different approach. At the next session, Yvette tentatively told the service user about what she had been thinking – she began by acknowledging and sharing her growing frustration that they didn't seem to be getting anywhere and that this had prompted her to think differently and try to imagine how his experiences had impacted on the process.

Through the process of critical reflection and taking these thoughts to the service user, Yvette was engaging in reflective practice. Within a couple of sessions, the situation was very different: the service user had appreciated Yvette's attempt to see things from his perspective and her acknowledgement that it had been increasingly difficult between the two of them. In turn, the service user began to share his experiences of prison life and offending and how this had shaped him – Yvette and he had a common ground in which to re-establish a working relationship and work in ways which facilitated the service user's involvement.

Comment

From reading Yvette's case study, a central theme emerges which is dominant in this book – that is, that practice matters. It matters how we do things – our actions matter to us and they matter to service users and their carers. Working well – doing our job with professional competency and with integrity – matters, otherwise we run the risk, at best, of adopting routine practice and, at worst, making tragic mistakes and devastating service users' lives. Social work is thus an active process of 'doing'. Given social work's far reaching remit into almost all aspects of our lives, from child care, to adoption, physical and mental ill health, developmental concerns, loss and death and old age, that process of 'doing', i.e. practice and behaviour, should be subject to review and evaluation. This is the role of critical thinking, but we can only think about our practice if we are aware of the ideas and the resulting beliefs and assumptions that guide our practice. Some of these ideas can be described as more formal knowledge, representing aspects of professional education or maybe agency expectations around policies or procedures which are intended to guide practice. Equally, formal knowledge can be understood as representing a particular approach to working, for instance, counselling, or the adoption of a particular theoretical perspective, such as feminism, or in Yvette's case, understanding labelling theory, to inform practice. These formal ideas and resulting beliefs can also be described as formal 'theories' that represent a framework which acts as an attempt to explain, and thus aid our understanding as they help us to begin to make sense of what is going on. But it is not just 'formal theories' of what we know which influence and guide our thoughts and practice. There are also 'informal theories' drawn from our personal experiences and developing 'practice wisdom' which shape our view of practice and the role of social work. All ideas, whether formal or informal, are based on assumptions and beliefs which guide and legitimate our view of what social work is and how to do the job. What this book concerns itself with is the process of developing our awareness or 'know-how' of these 'theories' and subjecting them to critical analysis so that we have a better understanding of their impact on our practice. In doing so, we learn to take more responsibility for the type of practice and worker we want to develop and you can see the integration of theory with practice most clearly in Chapter 5, where we can see how formal understandings of society can contribute towards our view of social work practice and the centrality of values and ethics in shaping our practice.

C H A P T E R   S U M M A R Y

In this opening chapter, you have been introduced to the main themes of this book, beginning with an exploration of different definitions of social work and their influence on social work practice. From this, we have considered the range of ideas and knowledge sources and resulting beliefs which influence our views and looked at what is meant by the term 'theory', seeing it as an exploratory framework which can aid our understanding and help us make sense of social work and its varied practice context. We have noted that there are competing explanations and how some explanations can become more dominant, and thus the idea of social constructionism and the use of the term 'discourse' are useful tools for considering the 'fluidity' of the idea that social work is a contested activity with competing ideas about its nature and purpose. Finally, the importance of critical thinking and reflective analysis have been identified as essential skills to develop as part of professional practice. In the following chapter we will explore in more detail how different social theories shape our view about the nature of society and a resulting discourse about 'individual rights and responsibilities', which in turn constructs a view about the nature and purpose of social work.

Brookfield, S (1987) *Developing critical thinkers.* Buckingham: Open University Press.
This is a useful and accessible text exploring what is meant by critical thinking and developing practical approaches for thinking critically.

Cree, V (2002) Social work and society. In Davies, M (ed.) *Companion to social work.* 2nd edition. Oxford: Blackwell Publishers Ltd.
An informative chapter that charts the historical development of social work, locating it within a discussion of different views about the nature of society.

Chapter 2

The relationship between theory and practice in social work

This chapter will help you to begin to meet the following National Occupational Standards.

Key Role 1: Prepare for, and work with individuals, families, carers, groups and communities to assess their needs and circumstances.

- Prepare for social work contact and involvement.

Key Role 2: Plan, carry out, review and evaluate social work practice, with individuals, families, carers, groups, communities and other professionals.

- Apply and justify social work methods and models used to achieve change and development, and improve life opportunities.

Key Role 5: Manage and be accountable, with supervision and support, for your own social work practice within your organisation.

- Manage and be accountable for your own work.

Key Role 6: Demonstrate professional competence in social work practice.

- Implement knowledge based social work models and methods to develop and improve your own practice.

It will also introduce you to the following academic standards as set out in the social work subject benchmark statements.

3.1.1 Social work services and service users.

The social processes (associated with, for example, poverty, unemployment, poor health, disablement, lack of education and other sources of disadvantage) that lead to marginalisation, isolation and exclusion and their impact on the demand for social work services.

3.1.2 The service delivery context.

The complex relationships between public, social and political philosophies, policies and priorities and the organisation and practice of social work, including the contested nature of these.

3.1.4 Social work theory.

The relevance of sociological perspectives to understanding societal and structural influences on human behaviour at individual, group and community levels.

The subject skills highlighted to demonstrate this knowledge in practice include:

- **Problem solving skills.**
- **Analysis and synthesis.**

Introduction

In looking at the relationship between theory and practice, we are considering the role of theory to informing practice in social work. Chapter 1 provided a definition of theory, describing it as representing a set of related ideas and assumptions which are drawn upon to help us explain something. A theory therefore represents an explanatory framework that aims to help us make sense of the situation in question. In aiming to help us 'make sense', theories help us structure and organise our thinking, enabling us to begin to make judgements about:

- what we think is going on;

- what can done to help, and why.

These two processes are related.

In beginning to identify what we think is going on, we are forming an assessment of the situation, but as part of our professional repertoire, we also need to identify what can be done to help and why. This second process refers to our intervention with service users and carers and, likewise, we need to be clear about the interventions adopted and that they will make a useful contribution to tackling the issues identified in 'what is going on'. In other words, there must be a relationship between our assessment (that is, our explanation and judgement about what is going on) and our intervention, which identifies what can be done and thereby justifies our thinking of 'what is going on'.

When acknowledged, therefore, these coherent ideas and assumptions are central to helping us make sense of our practice context and what we do. The emphasis on structuring and organising our thinking is, of course, part of the concept of critical thinking, and in this book is seen as central to effective social work. Professional practice cannot therefore be a 'scatter-gun' approach to 'what is going on' but instead, requires you to be clear about the ideas that are guiding your thinking and influencing your practice. Through the reflective process, you too can begin to answer the question of why you think these ideas are useful and valid in a particular instance or how these ideas help construct your understanding. The 'why' question therefore is an important part of being accountable – we should be able to justify and explain the ideas and decisions we make in our practice, but we can only begin to do this if we are clear about the ideas we draw upon in the first place. It is the reflective process of thinking about the ideas we draw upon which is the essence of *Understanding and using theory in social work* and is identified as a central component of effective professional practice in social work. This book emphasises the connection between thinking and doing, or theory and practice, and the need to recognise how each informs the other.

After reading this chapter, you should be able to:

- identify the distinction between formal and informal theories about social work;

- understand the contribution of social theories about the nature of society and how these contribute towards different views about the nature and purpose of social work;

- identify the pervasiveness of an individual rights and responsibilities discourse, and its impact on contemporary practice;

- consider an alternative conceptualisation about the nature of social work which relies on an empowerment perspective.

Using a social constructionist approach

Given the range of different practice contexts which exist in social work, such as work with older people, mental health and social work with children and families, coupled with the different reasons or difficulties presented in social work, we should recognise that inevitably there are different and competing explanations that can be utilised to help us make sense of what is going on and what can be done to help. This reminds us of the importance and contribution of 'social constructionism' (see Chapter 1). This approach is useful in helping us critically reflect about the ideas which inform and influence our interpretation of 'what is social work' and 'what is going on'. Social constructionism recognises that there are different constructions, or meanings about 'what is going on' which are influenced by important factors, such as context – for instance, the different practice contexts of social work – or social changes over time, the influence of legislation and different explanations about people's behaviour. These different factors influence the judgements we make. However, this approach is not intended to confuse or undermine your confidence in thinking about the ideas that inform your practice. On the contrary, social constructionism is a valuable tool in helping you think critically and reflectively about your practice and the ideas that influence it. Since it pays attention to important contextual factors, such as time and place and interpretation, it has a natural affinity with contemporary social work's interpersonal relationship base. In our work with service users and carers, in determining 'what is going on' or 'what the matter is' and 'what can be done and why', we are in the process of constructing a shared meaning about what the matter is and what can be done, in order to work effectively. In acknowledging different constructions or meanings about 'what the matter is', social constructionism draws attention to the process of interpretation and negotiation – which are not only key skills in social work, but equally in themselves, represent a process of social construction. From this approach, the construction of 'what we know' and how we 'make sense' are products of human meaning-making and reinforce the notion that meaning-making can be both complementary and contested. Howe (2002) recognises this as fruitful ground for social work theorising, since *social workers deal with people in social situations... rather than bemoan the number and range of theories, the practitioner needs to acknowledge that the diversity reflects the subtlety and complexity of the human condition* (pp83–4). Add to this the characterisation of social work as dealing with risk, uncertainty and complexity, then there is no getting away from the need for explanatory frameworks, or theories, in helping us make sense of what is going on. Inevitably therefore, theories can both compete with and be complementary to each other.

The notion of theories as representing competing frameworks of explanation to aid our understanding is suggestive of the possibility of adopting an eclectic approach to theorising which enables us to draw on a range of different ideas which together can help us to start to understand what might be going on and what the matter is. However, being an eclectic practitioner is not just about drawing on different theoretical explanations to help us make sense, but rather, being eclectic requires the use of critical thinking skills which seek to see how well these ideas go together in constructing a fuller understanding. When critically analysed, these ideas can serve as an explanation that seeks to help us make better sense. Theories therefore serve as a basis for meaning-making and lay the groundwork for our involvement with service users. However, the adoption of a social constructionist approach supports us in a critically reflective process of considering the importance of contextual factors which help shape and construct our ideas and their influence on our understanding and meaning-making.

Formal theories and their contribution to practice

Social work takes place in a social and political context. Therefore 'what social work is' and 'what social workers do' are influenced not only by ideas about the nature of society but equally, due to its mediating role between the state and the individual (Parton, 1996), social work's role is also influenced by debates about the role of the state in welfare and this represents its political context.

In this section, we look at different theories that seek to explain questions about the nature of society and the role of the individual within it. Formal theories represent what is probably most typically thought of as 'theory' by students and practitioners. 'Theory' is what is written down in texts and represents the ideas that are used to explain and help us understand questions about social work; whether, for example, the text attempts to help make sense of social work education, practice teaching or social work methods of intervention. Thus formal theories of social work represent the ideas which are used to help us make sense, provide explanations and challenge our thinking about social work. Since social work falls between the individual and society, we cannot avoid a consideration of theories about the nature of society, since social work is a socially mandated activity and will therefore reflect competing views about society's responsibility to vulnerable and socially excluded groups and individuals. It is possible therefore, to see why formal texts on social work that explore questions about the nature of social work can range from the type of education and training considered necessary, to debates about its various practice settings and questions about social policy for instance.

There are a range of different explanations or theories which social workers draw upon to help them make sense of the practice context of their work, or in their work with different service users. So, for instance, explanations about child and adult development can draw upon psychological and biological explanations about human growth and development, and readers can refer to Crawford and Walker's (2007) introductory text on human growth and development to develop their understanding. In addition, social workers are increasingly governed in their role by policies and procedures drawn from welfare legislation, and again, you will find it helpful to refer to texts such as *Using the law in social work* (2007) by Robert Johns, which will introduce you to the range of legislation that surrounds the task of social work.

However, in this book, I emphasise the importance of understanding questions about the nature of society, since social work performs a mediatory role between the individual and society and therefore, explanations about the nature of society influence our view or understanding about the role and purpose of social work. These represent sociological explanations about the nature of society and can be further described as 'formal theories' which emphasise a social explanation to help us make sense. Unsurprisingly there are different explanations about the nature of society and we will see that these different explanations have led to two main competing political views about the role of the state of the welfare. One view involves the belief that individuals should take primary responsibility for their welfare, independent of government involvement, while the alternative view argues that government has a responsibility to support its citizens, particularly those who are socially and materially disadvantaged. These two opposing views can be characterised as representing a discourse around 'rights and responsibilities' and will be discussed later on in this chapter. To begin with, however, we will look at the different explanations about the nature of society and how these views have influenced debates about the nature of social work.

There are three main theories which seek to explain questions about the nature of society. The first two are known as structuralist approaches, since they see society as largely shaping social life. However, they provide competing explanations based on a structural analysis of society and lead to contrasting views about the role of social work. In contrast, the third explanation is known as an interpretivist approach and draws on principles of social constructionism and is known as a social action theory. This approach is concerned more with explanations about action and meaning and is concerned with how individuals construct meaning about their social life. The unit of analysis is the individual and social life is seen as principally constructed through meaning.

Consensus theory

The first structuralist approach to be examined is the functionalist or consensus perspective on the nature of society. The consensus perspective advocates the importance of a common shared belief system which is learnt through a process of socialisation, begun initially through the family and continued within the education system and reinforced through the mass media. Thus we are all socialised into a common belief system, a kind of common culture with expectations about appropriate ways to behave. According to this view, we carry around with us ideas and expectations, reinforced through our socialisation and the mass media, about 'appropriate' ways to behave. These appropriate forms of behaving represent the norms and expectations of a given culture. While the functionalist perspective acknowledges movement and social diversity within cultures, it argues that there are dominant social norms and values with expectations of conformity – from this perspective, this explains the apparent social stability of many societies. Indeed it is this consensus about how we ought to behave that gives society its seeming stability. For those who support a functionalist perspective, the view about 'what social work is' and 'what social workers do' is likely to reflect a view about social work that reinforces a need for compliance to the dominant *status quo*. Dominelli (2002) describes this as a 'maintenance' perspective which views society as largely benign, and will yield a view about social work as largely a pragmatic activity, *usually passing on information about resources and possibilities. They are guided in their interventions by 'practice wisdom' or accumulated experience of 'what works'* (p4). Alternatively, Payne (2005) describes this as an 'individualist–reformist' (p9) view of social work, which seeks change at an individual level; difficulties either have practical solutions, as in the provision of a service, or individuals are encouraged and supported to deal more effectively with their situation, or are expected to reform in some way, for instance, in work with offenders or drug users. This is because individualist–reformist views about 'what social work is' seek a better fit between society and individuals, helping to maintain *people during any period of difficulties they may be experiencing, so they can recover stability* (p9). This approach does not seek social change but sees social work as contributing towards the maintenance of the dominant social system. Practice from this perspective will be orientated towards task-centred or systems theories and behavioural methods of intervention.

ACTIVITY 2.1

Reconsider the definition of social work, provided by the Department of Health, 2006, which describes social work as

a professional...and worthwhile job which focuses on improving people's well-being...helping vulnerable people to make crucial decisions to regain control of their lives. They may be parents and children who are struggling in the face of deprivation, disability or abusive behaviour; young adults who are finding it hard to handle the pressures of living independently; people with mental health problems; those with physical or learning disabilities; people with drug or alcohol problems; people suffering from HIV/AIDS; older people who need support or refugees and homeless people. (p4)

Consider how this view about the nature of social work supports a consensus view about the nature of society.

Comment

The Department of Health's definition can be described as representing an individualist–reformist (Payne, 2005) or maintenance view (Dominelli, 2002) about the nature of social work. Here, the social worker's focus is on the individual service user as the site for change or intervention and the worker is part of a jigsaw of welfare services concerned with improving people's well-being and linking them, or referring them to, other welfare agencies that may be more appropriate. The aim of intervention (or service provision) is to enable the person to regain control of their lives in order to recover stability (Payne, 2005). Interventions are based on reform (and the emphasis on social conformity, as part of a consensus view) or rehabilitation (through practical provision) rather than social change. Therefore the role of welfare services (of which social work is a part) can be described as originating from a consensus view about the nature of society and the role of the individual within it. We can see again the powerful influence of a consensus approach; it links into the belief about social work as a 'helping practical activity' that focuses on the individual to adapt or change, or through the use of practical assistance, the individual is enabled to manage more self-sufficiently. It is part of an individual rights and responsibilities discourse (discussed in more detail later in this chapter) and remains a powerful influence on contemporary social work practice, emphasising small-scale individual or incremental change rather than major social change. In this respect, you should realise the importance of 'context' (as part of a social constructionist approach) and the nature of the organisation in which you work, since organisations remain powerful moulders of social work practice (see Chapter 4, which explores the organisational context of contemporary social work practice).

Conflict theory

In contrast, the conflict perspective provides an alternative structuralist approach and, as the name suggests, adopts a more critical approach to understanding the structure of society and how social structures mediate social life. The conflict perspective argues that society is structured along lines of inequality, such as wealth, income and health, for instance, providing people with different life chances which can result in qualitatively different life experiences. The idea of a shared belief system is therefore highly doubtful since these social differences minimise opportunities for a shared common identity and instead create greater opportunities for social conflict between and within social groups. From this perspective social conflict is seen as both inevitable and a legitimate response to social inequality. The conflict perspective points to differences in life chances which produce qualitatively different life experiences. Such differences are likely to result in distinct and separate subgroups. In contrast to the consensus view, the conflict perspective argues that social differences are less the result of a failure in the socialisation process or an expression of individual deviancy or dysfunction, but instead represent differences in life chances and life experiences. The conflict approach argues that the idea of a shared and unifying common belief system is a myth designed and managed by ruling elites to represent their interests and maintain their powerful and privileged position.

If one supports a conflict analysis about the nature of society, then social work can represent one of two views: social work is either an agent of state control and used by the state to 'manage' and maintain the socially excluded and vulnerable, or social work can represent a radical activity, concerned to mobilise those socially excluded groups through group and community action.

Proponents of this first view, such as Jones (2001), Jordan (2000; 2001) and Stepney (2000) adopt a critical analysis of contemporary social work practice, pointing out that in Britain, the use of social work as a force of containment rather than alleviation goes back over 30 years. Jordan (2001) summarises this view when he states that statutory social work has increasingly been used as part of a mechanism for dealing with problems *of social polarisation, exclusion, poverty and disadvantage rather than part of a strategy for preventing them* (p140).

However, even those who are critical about social work's contemporary role are not unsympathetic to the view that social work should move beyond the role of state regulators and instead should be concerned to mobilise social change in favour of marginalised and vulnerable service users.

This represents the second view about 'what social work is' and describes an emancipatory approach, which Dominelli (2002) describes as one which has *an explicit commitment to social justice* (p4) in favour of disadvantaged and marginalised individuals and groups. For Payne (2005), this approach to social work represents a 'socialist–collectivist view' (p9). From this perspective, social work practice remains critical of the overarching social structure and seeks to challenge the established social order, which is seen to be biased in favour of elite groups. Instead practice is focused on achieving significant social change in favour of oppressed users groups. The practice of social work from a socialist–collectivist or emancipatory view will be orientated towards anti-oppressive and empowerment practices which seek social change, by helping individuals to *understand their situation, make connections between their personal plight and that of others, examine power relations and their impact on the specifics of their daily routines and acquire the knowledge and skills for taking control of their lives* (Dominelli, 2002, p4). Such a practice utilises techniques which seek to galvanise social change and politicise individuals, groups and communities. Thus through their relationship with the service user, the social worker seeks to raise their awareness, or 'consciousness raise' the service user, of their oppressed social position. Social work becomes a more overt political process – the worker acts as an agent of personal, and hence by implication, social change. As the service user gains an awareness of the nature of society and its oppressive social structures, they gain an understanding that their private difficulties are not simply their own, but parallel many other private lives. To use the commonly voiced feminist quote, 'the personal is the political'. The practitioner seeks to build alliances – here private difficulties are not individualised, but are seen to have their roots in oppressive social structures. Thus the focus of exploration shifts from the individual to the wider social structure and the analysis is political. Social work, seen from this perspective, acts as an agent of change, seeking to raise consciousness and develop alliances between individuals in order to promote collective action in pursuit of social change. Group work or community work, based on anti-discriminatory ideals, provides an example of a practice approach that is consistent with this approach.

In considering how a conflict approach towards understanding the nature of society can inform an approach to social work practice based upon emancipatory principles, turn to Chapter 5 and consider the case study of Maria and how she draws together her theoretical understanding of social theories and how these are used to inform her practice with a service user who has experienced domestic violence. You should notice again the influence of organisational context and how this impacts on Maria's work and supports a view of social work based upon an emancipatory approach.

In summary, the structuralist view supports two contrasting perspectives: the functionalist or consensus perspective and the conflict perspective. Both seek to provide an explanation about the nature of society by examining the structure of society, but they provide diametrically opposed explanations and influence different views about the nature and purpose of social work.

Interpretivist theory

The third approach to help us understand society is known as a social action theory and adopts an interpretivist or subjective view about the nature of society. The subjective view seeks to understand the social world by looking more at the interactions between social groups and individuals – it seeks to understand and analyse how individuals construct and interpret their social lives. As Payne (2005) states:

> *Society is separate from the individuals it contains, so we can be most effective by relating to and understanding how other human beings understand the world in relation to ourselves. Participation in human relationships means that we influence the world we are studying, and in turn our understandings about the world will influence how we behave.* (p55)

Principally, the subjective perspective looks to 'meaning' as the central feature which requires analysis, in other words, 'what does this action/behaviour mean to this individual?' and 'what are the ways meanings are constructed and interpreted?'

In social work, this perspective reveals a social constructionist approach to practice (Payne, 2005, p58) and is concerned to help the 'client' better understand their difficulties. It seeks an understanding that is meaningful to the 'client' and is guided by a commitment to 'progressive individualism'; that is, social work is seen as *seeking the best possible well-being for individuals, groups and communities in society, by promoting and facilitating growth and self-fulfilment* (p8). For many supporters of this perspective, this is the heart of social work – it is its therapeutic centre, the humanistic ideal of 'self-actualisation' or *client-centred practice* (Howe, 1987, p97) and is what Dominelli, (2002) calls the 'therapeutic helping' (p3) approach to social work practice. This approach focuses on individual change and psychological functioning as the basis for intervention. The relationship between the worker and 'client' is an important one and in many ways an intimate one, where the client shares their concerns and distress with the worker and where the client seeks to gain 'insight' into their troubles to an extent where the client feels able to function or manage satisfactorily. The interpretivist seeks change through personal insight and the establishment of a therapeutic relationship between worker and client, such as is typical of a counselling approach. Like the functionalist perspective, neither practice approach seeks to threaten the integrity of the social order. It is this dynamic between worker and client that according to Payne (2005) gives social work its reflexive nature, as the worker helps the client to modify their understanding of 'what is going on' while at the same time, the client influences the worker's understanding and experience of 'what is going on'. For this reason, Payne (2005) describes this approach to social work as part of a 'reflexive–therapeutic view' (pp8-9).

In terms of social work practice, an interpretivist approach will yield a view about the nature of social work that emphasises meaning-making and understanding, which as suggested, is typical of counselling approaches. Examples of practice settings are 'therapeutic communities' such as residential units working with people experiencing problematic substance use, such as alcohol or drug dependency, or units dealing with people experiencing eating disorders. The therapeutic element emphasises group membership and individual support, where group support and dynamics are explored and facilitated by group members or experiences are explored and meaning sought in individual work. Techniques include talking, but more creative methods to help meaning-making and expression may be used, such as varied art work, creative writing such as poetry or keeping a journal, or, in work with young children, play therapy may be used.

It is a more inductive approach to knowledge building and understanding, in contrast to the structuralist perspective which adopts a 'top-down' or deductive approach to understanding the individual's behaviour. The structuralist approaches see individuals as largely influenced by the social environment whereas the interpretivist looks towards meaning-making and how our ideas and beliefs are constructed and influence our behaviour.

A social constructionist approach is therefore useful in helping us make sense of how formal theories on the nature of society help to construct our understanding of the relationship between the individual and society. Further, we can see these different social theories also influence our view about the nature and purpose of social work. However, we also know that social work takes place in different settings and therefore we can appreciate the importance of context that is emphasised in a social constructionist approach. In particular, the agency context helps to construct our role which is mediated by factors such as legislation and policy directives, including performance indicators and financial constraints as well as the influence of other factors, such as workloads, service provision resources and service user needs. Such factors show up the importance of interpretation and negotiation in constructing meaning and helping us to make sense of questions about the nature and purpose of social work.

How social theories can be used by social workers

We can see that these three formal social theories provide us with competing explanations about the nature of society, but you should note in these theories the contrast between an interest in social structures (such as characterises the structuralist approaches) and the emphasis on meaning-making and how this guides social action, as in the interpretivist view. They therefore represent views on a continuum from the interpretivist to the structuralist position. However, rather than see each view as competing against one another, I would argue that since they are theories and each seeks to aid our understanding, they can all contribute towards a fuller understanding of the complexities of social life. Social theories give us an explanation about the relationship between the individual and society and therefore a way of beginning to understand how social problems may occur and that this can be understood as representing a disjunction between the individual and their social context.

ACTIVITY **2.2**

Try to identify at least one advantage of these three theories in helping you to understand more fully questions about the nature of society and the role of the individual within it.

Comment

The consensus view is useful in explaining the seeming stability and order of our society and how this can be explained as a result of the process of socialisation and dominant norms and expectations that influence our behaviour; the conflict view allows us to see commonalities of experience across different individuals, such as poverty or the experience of racism, that point to social processes rather than just an individual explanation; and the interpretivist approach allows for a sense of 'agency' or personal control, and that we are not tied to social structures, but that we have the freedom and ability to create, change and influence our social environment and construct alternative meanings for our lives. All three theories therefore can be used to develop and enrich our understanding of social life by helping us make sense of people's behaviour by providing explanations and challenges to our thinking about the nature and purpose of social work.

Formal theories of any discipline should serve as the bedrock to any professional's knowledge; if we go back to the definition of theory as representing a framework of understanding, helping us to make sense and providing an explanation, then clearly we need an understanding and appreciation of the formal ideas and beliefs which underpin and help construct an understanding of social work. We have already seen that these ideas and beliefs represent competing explanations and this adds to the ambiguity about social work's role and purpose. However, a central benefit of formal theories is that they are written down and open to interpretation and debate – if it is written down, we have time to digest the argument and compare it with other views, or perspectives; it has the advantage of being open to debate and analysis and challenge and ideas refined or extended.

ACTIVITY **2.3**

Look back to Activity 1.1 (in Chapter 1) and how you described social work.
- *How far does your description represent a view about social work that has been described by Dominelli (2002) or Payne (2005)?*

ACTIVITY **2.3** *continued*

- *How far does your view about social work also represent a view about the nature of society and the role of the individual within it?*
- *Where would you place yourself on the continuum of structuralist to interpretivist views and does your view about social work practice reflect one of these views?*

Comment

While I can recognise the pervasiveness of the consensus view on the nature of society, I tend to adopt a critical analysis about social structures and therefore am more sympathetic towards a conflict view about society. However, my preference for a social constructionist approach means that I also favour an interpretivist analysis and therefore look towards the relationship between worker and service user as a basis for meaning-making and one which emphasises the importance of personal agency. My view about the nature of social work therefore encompasses an emancipatory approach that stresses the importance of the interpersonal relationship between service user and the worker. I explore this in more detail in Chapter 5 when I examine the use of a strengths-based approach in social work that is guided by principles of social change in favour of an emancipatory approach.

Individual rights and responsibilities discourse

Different explanations about the nature of society influence our attitude about the nature and purpose of social work. In other words, they reveal different conceptualisations about the role and purpose of welfare. We can now turn to consider an influential conceptualisation about the role and purpose of welfare that has contributed to a powerful discourse around 'rights and responsibilities' which favours a focus on individual rights.

The consensus perspective on the nature of society most closely corresponds to a view about the role of the state in welfare that emphasises a residual role for the state. This view supports a discourse around individual rights and responsibilities that favours and promotes individual responsibility over and above a collective approach. Such a view is characteristic of anti-collectivist or neo-liberal approaches to welfare, such as have typified British and American approaches to welfare over the last 30 years. This residualist attitude considers an extended role for the state in welfare as fundamentally threatening to the economic and social well-being of a free market economy and instead believes that individuals should plan for their future, (i.e. be self-reliant and 'responsible') rather than rely on state-funded welfare provision. However, this is not to deny a role for the state in welfare, but this should remain as a last resort, a safety net intended for those with no other means of support. Parton (1996, p8) defines this as a rejection of what he terms 'welfarism', that is, the belief that universal social services are the best way of maximising welfare in modern society and further, the rejection of the view that the state is the most effective way of progressing welfare for all.

For proponents of a residual or anti-collectivist approach, an overdeveloped state welfare system has been responsible for inducing dependency, demoralisation and irresponsibility among its users and sapping their initiative. This view supports a belief about individual culpability – it is the individual's fault if they require support. Although state welfare can be provided, this is only in the short term and is seen as a means of encouraging individual responsibility and minimising their dependency. In all this reinforces a dominant discourse around 'rights and responsibilities' which favours the idea and perpetuates the belief that individual rights are more important than collective rights and obligations and that the individual should take primary responsibility for their welfare rather than rely on state provision.

Although it is possible to trace these changes in attitude about welfare as originating in government policies (and first appearing in Britain under the Thatcher Conservative government, 1979–90), Wilson (1998) suggests otherwise. She argues that welfare changes in Britain are less to do with the result of government policies (regardless of their political or ideological foundations) but are more the result of a worldwide movement away from collective action towards the individual marketisation of all aspects of social life (Wilson, 1998, p51). In order words, Wilson (1998) identifies the seemingly worldwide domination of an economic system based on capitalism and free trade policies, that is, economic neo-liberalism. The globalisation of neo-liberal economic policy has led to worldwide attempts to cut state-funded welfare while at the same time increasing state-controlling management structures alongside encouraging greater consumer choice and consumption, that is, an individual's ability to purchase goods and services. In Britain, even the New Labour government (first elected in 1997), have embraced this ideological trend and rejected a core value of the political left, namely a belief in the role of the state as the main provider of welfare, with obvious implications for social work.

Under New Labour, the government has reduced the role of the state in welfare, instead supporting increasing privatisation within traditionally thought of state services, such as health and social care and education, alongside increasing consumer choice. In Britain, it is the likes of New Deal schemes and SureStart programmes which are driving through the changes on conditional welfare, with social workers left to pick up the residual cases – either those too vulnerable for social participation (and thus social work provides the 'safety net') or those deemed unwilling to co-operate. Particularly in these latter circumstances, the discourse about rights and responsibilities supports a partnership between the state and those individuals requiring intervention. For Powell (2003), this marks a shift away from *a patterned to a process-driven distribution. In other words, benefits and services may no longer be delivered simply on the basis of a criterion such as need, but might be varied to accord with behaviour* (p104). He goes on to give the example of 'welfare to work' policies and public housing evictions for 'anti-social behaviour' as evidence of conditional state welfare balanced against an emphasis on individual responsibility. The moral undertones of the 'rights and responsibilities' discourse become obvious as we see increasing state attempts to regulate social life in terms of social compliance and control. New Labour's social policies are less concerned with promoting social equality but are designed more to promote social inclusion (through employment) and a 'civil society' with its 'tough on the causes' and 'anti-social' strategies alongside welfare entitlement premised on a 'no rights without responsibility' rhetoric. For New Labour, *social inclusion is viewed as facilitating social cohesion rather than addressing inequality . . . the overall focus is not on the causes but on the effects of exclusion* (Burden and Hamm, 2000, p197).

The individual rights and responsibilities discourse represents a body of ideas and beliefs which have become increasingly established as 'common-sensical' and an accepted world view. It is not just tied, as might be your first thought, to a conservative political ideology, but has been just as eagerly embraced in Britain's New Labour government. The pervasiveness of this discourse therefore goes beyond political and national boundaries but represents, as Wilson (1998) says, a worldwide movement away from collective action with a focus on structural inequalities, towards a focus on the individual in society which emphasises personal responsibility and culpability.

The pervasive nature of this discourse highlights the importance of critical thinking and an ability to interrogate these influential ideas and their impact – that is, it calls to mind a need for 'discourse analysis'. As Healy (2005, p9) states, this draws attention to *the conditional, changeable character of social work* and thus a need *to recognise the diversity of social work practices.* In addition, the discourse of rights and responsibilities highlights the ambiguous role of social workers as administrators of social policies, as they straddle the 'space' between the individual and society.

> ## ACTIVITY 2.4
>
> *Having considered the prevalence of the individual rights and responsibilities discourse in social work, and the alternative discourse of empowerment, what criticisms do you think an empowerment approach would make of the terms 'consumer' and 'partnership'?*

Comment

Healy (2005) uses the term 'neo-classical economic discourse' and states that *few social work commentators support [this] discourse* (p32), yet its pervasiveness is evident in social work practice. In particular, the emphasis on an individual focus elevates the primacy of the individual and assumes we all have the same social opportunities. For instance, in emphasising 'consumer choice' and 'partnership', key themes in this discourse, this implies that the 'consumer' has a choice over service provision and interventions – in other words, the health and social care 'market' offers a wide range of services that can meet and respond to the varied needs of the individual consumer. Secondly, partnership implies an equal relationship between service provider and consumer, by-passing the contentious nature of 'statutory involvement'. Instead, the rights and responsibilities discourse plays to a moral high ground that we are individually responsible for our social predicament and therefore in areas of (accepted) social transgression, we must inevitably accept the consequences of statutory involvement and what this might entail. The individual focus militates against a consideration of the structural processes which impact on and mediate our life experiences.

The empowerment approach

Drawing on the work of Mills (1997, p13), I have previously described a discourse as having *meaning, force and effect* and that it is played out in institutions and social contexts that help maintain and reinforce its circulation. However, we also know that a discourse can serve to exclude alternative understandings that can operate in contrast and opposition. In this section, we look at an alternative discourse that challenges the focus on individual rights and responsibilities.

The empowerment approach is a generic or collective term used to describe those views about the nature of social work as being concerned to promote social change and achieve greater social justice through individual and collective strategies. It is therefore part of an alternative discourse that shifts the focus of exploration away from individual culpability and responsibility and instead incorporates an analysis of structural processes in order to enrich our understanding of the difficulties individuals and communities may face. It looks towards social change based on collective rights and responsibilities rather than the focus on individual rights and responsibilities and is therefore part of a critical discourse to understanding individual and social problems.

From this perspective, social work is part of a socially emancipatory project (Dominelli, 2002) and is concerned with the promotion of social equality or social justice in favour of those groups and individuals who can be described as vulnerable, disadvantaged or marginalised – that is, those groups and individuals who typically make up the majority of users of social services. It therefore supports social change in this direction and looks towards alternative explanations to understand people's behaviour, vulnerabilities and disadvantages, seeking out those explanations which move beyond simplistic notions of individual culpability. As an alternative discourse it *offers different interpretations about the nature of clients' needs, expert knowledge, the nature of the social work role and most specifically, the kinds of 'help' or intervention that will best address the concerns and issues facing service users* (Healy, 2005, p9).

This approach argues in favour of explanations that move away from pathologising the individual, but instead looks to support individuals and groups to gain a sense of control over their circumstances and to live lives which are socially valued from a social justice perspective. The concept of social exclusion therefore, is a valid one for social work – we deal in the stuff of social exclusion, with marginalised, disadvantaged and vulnerable individuals. But the term 'social exclusion' represents multiple deprivation resulting from a lack of personal and social, as well as political and financial, opportunities, and therefore the strategies needed to support and encourage social inclusion need to be varied and adaptable. Critically as well, we need to consider the type of society or community we are encouraging and supporting inclusion (back) into.

At a personal or individual level, 'social inclusion' can be better understood as 'personal integration'. We need to ask ourselves how we can support the development and growth of resilience and positive self-esteem, that is, the personal qualities that support the development of psychological health. Thus we need to ask ourselves how we can support those people or individuals whose behaviour or lifestyles are not socially valued, for instance, asylum seekers, people with disabilities, offenders, immigrants, ethnic minorities and drug users.

The concept of social exclusion is particularly useful when discussed from an empowerment or social justice perspective since it provides a broader context from which to begin to understand multi-dimensional disadvantage. So it is not just traditional groups, like the poor and long-term unemployed, who are at risk from the negative effects of social exclusion, there is increasing instability among affluent groups as well. Viewed like this, there is scope for acknowledging the dimensions of social exclusion as a phenomenon that can cut across all social groups and result in increased social and psychological instability for anyone (Williams, 1998). Williams (1998) goes on to warn of the dangers of focusing on socially excluded groups, rather than causes, stressing that the representation of these groups as 'homogenous groupings' can trivialise differences among groups as well as the different forms of exclusion involved. As social life grows increasingly complex and we move away from fixed forms of identity based on say, sexuality, social class, job status, marriage and even national boundaries, the risk of social exclusion becomes higher for everyone, but more importantly, the effects and meaning of social exclusion are equally varied and have different consequences for each of us.

The strategies therefore, which are required to support a long-term unemployed 35-year-old white male are different to those required for a man the same age who has recently been made redundant from his banking job of 15 years. How we deal with these uncertainties owes as much to life chances (which tend to favour a structural explanation) as they do to our life experiences, which are mediated by more variable factors, such as personal and communities resources. In tackling issues of social exclusion, those of us committed to ideals of social justice are faced with a fundamental challenge – *how do we bring together a commitment to universal values and universal access to rights, with a commitment to recognising the peculiarities of difference?* (Williams, 1998, p17). If social work wants to play a more significant role in tackling issues of social inequality, then it needs to reassert and reaffirm its commitment to empowering perspectives and the alternative discourse it represents. This is a responsibility for all key players; social work education; students and practitioners; service users; and professional bodies, such as the General Social Care Council and the British Association of Social Workers, for example. Social work has always occupied an ambiguous role, acting as a safety net to support the vulnerable and 'needy' as well as being used as a mechanism to control and manage 'deviant' behaviour. Our ambiguous role has been variously described over time as representing the 'care/control' dichotomy, or in relation to service users, 'the deserving or undeserving' and most recently 'the socially excluded'. Acting alone, we are not responsible for the state of social work, but we do have a responsibility to think critically about what kind of society we want our work to contribute to. As part of an alternative discourse, the empowerment perspective encourages this process.

Although contemporary welfare is premised on notions of individual rights and responsibilities or conditional welfare, the establishment of a working relationship (or even 'partnership' as the preferred term) is still crucial between the worker or service provider, and the recipient, or service user. This is where social work can claim a stronghold, as the development of interpersonal skills has always been considered as being at the heart of social work practice, what Payne (2005) refers to as the *reflexive therapeutic* view, or what Dominelli (2002) terms the *therapeutic helping approach*. It is these skills that represent the strengths of social work and provide opportunities for flexible and creative forms of practice that are grounded in meaning for the service user and thus provide and support opportunities for change. We will look in more detail at this process in Chapter 5.

Informal theories and their contribution to practice

So far in this chapter, we have looked at the contribution of formal theories to understanding the practice context of social work, as well as a consideration of the influences of discourses and how they help construct our view of the social work role. In this final section we return to the issue of 'theory' but this time consider the influence of informal theories and how they shape our practice.

In contrast to formal theories, informal theories are more difficult to pin down and typically represent taken-for-granted ideas and beliefs that are culturally and professionally reinforced. Socially and culturally, for instance, informal ideas about how to behave are gleaned from the way we have been socialised, and are reinforced by our familial and social relationships, and culturally through the mass media, for instance, in newspapers, books, plays, and from watching the television – they all deal with the stuff of life, and the stuff of life is what makes up social work as well. So while we get formal explanations for people's behaviour, such as sociological or psychological theories, these ideas also get translated into taken-for-granted or 'common-sense' ideas, such as explanations about so-called 'anti-social behaviour' which can be spoken about in terms of individual's 'not being brought up properly'. Such expressions are not necessarily at odds with formal theories, such as a functionalist perspective, which might emphasise poor socialisation within the family, or say a psychological perspective, which might look to understand the behaviour in terms of 'attachment' issues between the parent and child. We may also explain 'anti-social behaviour' as 'unsurprising' and as a legitimate response to high levels of social deprivation, rather than focus on the individual as a site of change. Such a view is more representative of a conflict analysis of society when understood at a formal level. However, an inherent danger with informal theories is that they tend to be based on unquestioned assumptions. Such assumptions may unwittingly reinforce dominant norms and expectations about 'appropriate' ways to behave. Even if we support a functionalist perspective on society and the purpose of social work, our interventions with service users should still be based on rigorous assessment informed by a critical knowledge base that is adaptive towards service users and carers and their varied situations.

Informal theories exist at a practice level as well. So theories of 'how *to do* social work' can also be understood and be characterised by 'word of mouth' ideas and beliefs, perhaps spoken by a practitioner and eagerly appreciated by the student social worker on placement, or the newly qualified worker, keen to appear competent and eager to 'learn' the 'real job' of social work. 'Word of mouth' teaching can also be understood as 'practice wisdom' or 'practice experience', passed down by the experienced to the novice; they are the 'short-cuts', or practice examples of working with particular service users, or a 'handy tip' on dealing with the paperwork. At best, these examples allow the novice to look upon the experienced worker as a positive role model and to appreciate and learn from the tips that are passed to him or her to enable a better grasp of the job. At worst, however, practice wisdom can be a by-word for 'burnt out and cynical' – stuck in a rut of familiar patterns and full of stereotypical anecdotes about 'types' of service users and an over-reliance on appeals to 'common sense'. In contrast to formal theories, informal theories are more colloquial; they may have their origin in formal theories, but they have become 'watered down' and influenced by experience. Of course 'the experience' is the act of 'doing' social work – it is the experience of practice that helps shape and refine our knowledge and belief systems and increases the capacity to work effectively with service users. However, experience can also be our downfall – the more experience we have, the greater the danger of familiarity which can foster routine and uncritical practice. Therefore, the reflective practitioner and student is one who is prepared to think critically about what they do by considering:

- what are the bases of the ideas which inform my practice?

- are there alternative explanations for understanding what is going on?

- what have I learnt about my practice?

- what strategies can I develop to improve my work?

Reflective thinkers interrogate their practice, their actions and the ideas that guide their practice and perhaps most importantly, are prepared to change their behaviour or practice and are committed to a process of attempting to improve their practice. Our practice experience should improve our work. However, one cannot just assume that experienced practitioners are necessarily the most effective unless they remain committed to an active process of reflection which manifests itself in improved practice. As a result of the demands of practice, (formal) theories can become more malleable precisely because we are working in the 'real world', but this should not undermine their validity. As stated, theories represent frameworks, they are attempts to explain, to help us make sense of and begin to understand what is going on, and they can provide competing explanations. It becomes even more important therefore for the practitioner to be rigorous in their thinking and the applicability of theories – that is, the whole range of ideas and beliefs that inform their thinking and influence their practice. We know we carry both formal and informal assumptions and ideas around with us, and that they will likely influence our behaviour towards service users. If these assumptions and ideas remain unquestioned and unchanged, we run the risk of moving towards routinised uncritical practice, which at worst could manifest itself in dangerous practice. Professional practice should be based on assessment skills which draw on all our sources of knowledge, which include formal and informal theories, research and practice experience, in order to help us make sense of what is going on and to determine what the most appropriate form of intervention is – otherwise, what makes us different from the lay person if we are not prepared to consider our assumptions and be reflective about the ideas (formal and informal) that guide our practice?

RESEARCH SUMMARY

In their research, Osmond and O'Connor (2004) examined how social work practitioners express and explain what they know and use in their practice to another (p678). This is important not only in terms of what it means to be 'a professional' and the use of knowledge (and therefore part of the process of being accountable), but the capacity to articulate...practice knowledge should also improve the likelihood of promoting quality service delivery to clients (p678). They go on to identify four main ways that social work practitioners express their knowledge understanding in practice. These are:

- *case examples, stories and metaphors, whereby practitioners' knowledge and understanding are embedded in the example;*

- *understandings which resemble existing knowledge, but are not formally labelled as such by practitioners, who instead tend to offer a speculative or tentative title which could easily be dismissed and discarded (p685) by researchers or educators;*

- *reformulated or synthesised knowledge – here the practitioner may generate a new understanding of practice theory based upon their practice experience and formal explanations – this suggests a pluralistic or eclectic approach that has been generated over time and therefore a formalised title of their understanding or knowledge may not exist;*

- *explicitly named understanding.*

Osmond and O'Connor's research is informative because it suggests that the articulation of knowledge understanding by practitioners may not be readily recognised by researchers, educators or practice teachers. This is because practitioners' knowledge and understanding are less likely to be articulated and expressed through formal or theoretical language and may therefore reinforce a dominant view that practitioners do not utilise formalised knowledge in practice, raising concerns that social work activity is unsystematic and potentially unprofessional (p681).

From their research, the authors identify three important issues for consideration for educators and practitioners. Firstly, educators and researchers need to recognise the diversity of knowledge communication utilised by practitioners – what the authors refer to as practice language. Secondly, following on from this, there is the danger that knowledge will be missed if the unique ways in which practitioners talk about their

RESEARCH SUMMARY *continued*

work is not recognised; and thirdly, greater attention should be given to helping students and practitioners articulate what they know. The prime objective is to promote clearer practice articulations with stronger knowledge links and to see this as a non-negotiable component of professional behaviour (p689).

The following case study draws out some of the themes discussed so far regarding the use of informal and formal theories of social work and their impact on practice.

CASE STUDY

Fiona's second-year placement was in a Children and Families team based in a busy town centre. The town had a well-known estate that was characterised by high levels of social deprivation, associated with poverty, unemployment, vandalism and drug use. Unsurprisingly, much of the team's work originated from the estate. Within a few weeks, Fiona had proved herself to be a very able student with a good grasp of the department's procedures and paperwork and good interpersonal skills with service users and the team. However, Fiona found her experience increasingly frustrating – several of the team seemed to over-rely on negative comments about their service users, referring to them as 'wasters' or 'spongers' and that it doesn't matter what you do, it doesn't make a difference, and warned Fiona that once she'd been in the job as long as them, she wouldn't be so idealistic. When challenged, they laughed it off as a defence mechanism. One team member told Fiona to 'lighten up' – you don't need to take everything so seriously – we're all just trying to do a difficult job. In supervision, she raised her concerns with her practice teacher (PT), explaining she felt like some team members had a tabloid-like mentality towards the service users which was offensive and unprofessional.

While the PT acknowledged Fiona's concerns, she also set her some homework and asked her to think about what she had learnt so far from her colleagues, as well as thinking of alternative explanations that could be used to explain service users' behaviour rather than a reliance on stereotypes. At the next supervision session, Fiona discussed her work. She acknowledged that she had learnt a lot so far from the team – they had shown her 'the ropes', shown her how to complete the many pieces of paperwork; she had observed their interactions with other professionals and overheard them on the phone, and seen them working with service users. Fiona had gained confidence from her observations and learnt a lot of jargon and 'tricks of the trade' – more so, she acknowledged than she learnt at college – useful expressions for instance, or writing styles required for different reports. However, she pointed out, she couldn't understand why they resorted to such dismissive comments about some service users. Fiona had researched alternative explanations, such as sociological and psychological perspectives which provided a more credible and less offensive explanation for drug use and deviant behaviour, for example. Her PT pointed out the concept of 'practice wisdom' and its benefits and some of the drawbacks, just as Fiona had identified, and she asked Fiona to consider why some of the team relied on stereotypical assumptions, rather than a more evidence-based or formal analysis. Fiona thought, and explained that no doubt it was due to pressure of work – it was a busy office and the team all had large case-loads – perhaps exclaimed Fiona, they don't have time to think…I guess they don't feel like picking up a textbook when they get home! she mused.

Over the remaining time of the placement, Fiona was able to acknowledge to the team the benefits of their experience and they in turn acknowledged that their comments about service users hid a more complex explanation than their taken-for-granted assumptions, which they acknowledged, was dismissive and unfair.

Fiona's final placement took place in a newly formed Youth Offending Team (YOT) and consisted of a team who described themselves as highly motivated and committed to working with young people. Fiona was impressed with the team; they had a team statement which was displayed in the office and in the waiting room, which conveyed the ethos of the team and a positive image about young people and the choices available to them. In the team, there was a commitment to ongoing professional development; when team members went on courses, they had to prepare a paper and give a 15-minute presentation on their return, demonstrating what the course was about and what they had learnt. The team supported the idea that they all had things to learn from each other and that information should be shared and discussed and that professional practice demanded an atmosphere of continuous engagement. The office also had a quiet room with a bookshelf of books and journals and professional magazines – workers could retreat to this room to complete paperwork, or read. Fiona especially enjoyed her final placement – in contrast to her first placement, there was an atmosphere of continuing professional development – here, established team members didn't talk about having 'seen it all before' in a resigned way, but instead, when bogged down by the challenges and restraints of the work, acknowledged the demands of the job. They did not seek to 'blame the victim' but could identify alternative explanations and often shared complex or 'stuck' cases with one another. When Fiona talked to her university tutor, she was able to identify the use of formal theories in her placement and that in the YOT, she had found a workplace where theory and practice were dynamic and in support of each other, enabling the team to work creatively and purposively with their service users.

Comment

Fiona's case study highlights that theory and practice are not two opposing forces that have no impact on each other: ideas and beliefs very much influence our actions and so theory is very much at the heart of our practice. When we refer to informal theory and practice wisdom, we are not always conscious of our ideas; some of them are so taken for granted and well rehearsed that we feel we practise instinctively. At best, in these cases we practise with competence and expertise. However, at worst, this can descend into routine practice which rests on taken-for-granted assumptions and which can represent common-sense perspectives which can reinforce the *status quo*. Social work becomes a job that we no longer need to think about, it is a job which has been done before and the familiarity is well established. What Fiona observed in her first placement was routine practice, but in the privacy of the office, away from the service users, revealed itself also to be riddled with negative stereotypes and assumptions about service users and carers – the familiarity of the work had dulled their senses so that they were unable to see alternative perspectives and consider alternative explanations. The team seemed to feed off each other, reinforcing negative comments, involving themselves in routine and unengaging work. In contrast, Fiona's final placement revealed the benefit of drawing on formal theories in order to understand and explain the complexities of people's behaviour and their situation. In the office, the team were familiar with, or at least had access to, material which provided rich explanations about deviancy and youth offending, which drew on sociological explanations about anti-social behaviour and labelling, or peer pressure or family breakdown, or behavioural perspectives which threw light on challenging disruptive behaviour, or psychological explanations about resilience and vulnerability and promotion of protective factors. The team enjoyed the challenge of talking about their role and the complexity of 'doing social work', i.e. practice and working with a stigmatised group of service users, such as offenders. Inevitably there were times when the team become demoralised, but the open commitment to engaging with the work through critical discussion and analysis meant that the team maintained a vibrancy that had been missing from Fiona's first placement.

C H A P T E R   S U M M A R Y

In this chapter we have located social work as representing a mediating role between society and the individual and therefore explored the contribution of formal theories about the nature of society and how these contribute towards views about the nature and purpose of social work as well as a consideration of informal theories and their contribution to practice.

We have also explored what I describe as the pervasive influence of an individual rights and responsibilities discourse which has permeated contemporary constructions of social work and the emphasis on individual responsibility. However, since discourses compete and exclude, we have also looked at the development of an empowerment perspective which offers an alternative discourse to the one on individual rights and responsibilities, and instead stresses 'collective action', which has always been a central (albeit contested) concern for social work practice.

Engaging with both the informal and formal ideas which guide and influence our practice, makes for a practice which is dynamic and creative, as you are enabled to think about the various explanations and ideas which guide your practice or seek out alternative explanations or constructions when your work seems 'stuck' or when you are challenged in your thinking.

The key is a critical analysis of these ideas and beliefs and in the best circumstances, requires both an individual and a team commitment to re-examining work practices and the benefits or limitations of alternative views.

FURTHER READING

British Journal of Social Work (2001) *Social work and New Labour: End of the first term.* 31 (4). Buckinghamshire: Open University Press.
This is an informative special issue and contains a collection of articles from different authors on New Labour's first term and the impact on social work.

Healy, K (2005) *Social work theories in context.* Basingstoke: Palgrave.
A useful book which emphasises the application of theory to practice and considers key discourses, including legal and economic, that inform current practice.

Chapter 3

Values and ethics in social work

A C H I E V I N G   A   S O C I A L   W O R K   D E G R E E

This chapter will begin to help you meet the following National Occupational Standards.

Key Role 6: Demonstrate professional competence in social work practice.

- Exercise and justify professional judgements.
- Work within the principles and values underpinning social work.
- Identify and assess issues, dilemmas and conflicts that might affect your practice.
- Reflect on outcomes.

It will also introduce you to the following academic standards as set out in the social work subject benchmark statements.

3.1.3 Values and ethics.

- The nature, historical evolution and application of social work values.
- Aspects of philosophical ethics relevant to the understanding and resolution of value dilemmas and conflicts in both interprofessional and professional contexts.
- The conceptual links between codes defining ethical practice, the regulation of professional conduct and the potential conflicts generated by the codes held by different professional groups.

This chapter will also help you follow the General Social Care Council Code of Practice for Social Care Workers and the British Association of Social Workers Code of Ethics for Social Work.

Introduction

Values and ethics lie at the heart of social work practice and therefore represent another dimension of the sources of knowledge we draw upon to inform our practice. While the social work literature may emphasise the acquisition of knowledge and skills necessary for effective practice, Banks (2006) suggests this is an artificial delineation, although it can be helpful *so long as it is not implied that knowledge can be value-free, or that legal and technical decisions can be made without recourse to ethics* (p11).

For students and practitioners of social work, our choice of values shapes and determines our actions and behaviours towards service users and the context in which we practise. Parrott (2006) emphasises the inherent ethical components of social work by describing it as a *practical-moral activity* that holds *a privileged position within the public services in working with people who often experience profound problems and significant crises in their lives which require practical solutions but have important moral consequences* (p3). This means our behaviours and actions have the potential to improve people's situation and therefore can be described as having a 'positive outcome'. Conversely, our behaviours and actions have the potential to damage and do harm and therefore can be described as having a 'negative outcome'. Given that social work is a purposeful activity, that is, we are expected to do something, this emphasises the need for an ethical approach in our practice. Thus we need to be clear about the values and ethics which influence and guide our behaviour and this calls to mind a number of interrelated factors to consider, including:

- the influence of our personal values and their impact on our practice;

- our view about the nature and purpose of social work;

- professional values and professional codes of ethics and practice;

- the influence of ethical theories in determining how we ought to behave as professional social workers;

- components of ethical decision-making.

These are not abstract considerations but represent some of the fundamental considerations that we need to be aware of in our practice as social workers, reinforcing the centrality of values and ethics in social work. We will therefore explore these issues in more detail throughout this chapter, but to begin with, I want to clarify what is meant by the terms 'values' and 'ethics'.

Defining values and ethics

Values and ethics are frequently used interchangeably, but as Loewenberg and Dolgoff (1992) point out, refer to different concepts.

Values are suggestive of general preferences and tend to describe what is 'good and desirable' shaping our beliefs and attitudes. In turn, values also have an affective quality, that is, they provoke our emotions, influencing which goals or behaviour we perceive as 'good' or worthwhile, or conversely, those behaviours we perceive negatively. Used in a professional context, however, the term 'belief' reflects the view that values are more than simply preferences or opinions (Banks, 2006). Adopting Banks' approach, social work values refer to a:

> *range of beliefs about what is regarded as worthy or valuable in a social work context (general beliefs about the nature of the good society, general principles about how to achieve this through actions and the desirable qualities or character traits of professional practitioners).* (p7)

We can see in Banks' definition that questions about the nature of society and the purpose of social work are interrelated, as we saw in Chapter 2, and this reflects value questions about the nature of society and the social work role. Equally, values influence our behaviour and this refers to the ends for which we act, or the purpose of the actions we undertake. We will see later in the chapter when we consider the subject of ethical theories, that this reflects significant differences in approaches to ethical decision-making that concern whether the ends (that is, the purpose or goal) ever justify the means. Finally, Banks' comments about the qualities or character traits of the practitioner reflect a growing interest in the role of virtue or character in how we behave. This suggests that it is not just the action or behaviour that needs to be considered when we talk about values and ethics, but that the person carrying out that behaviour is also subject to scrutiny. So, how we behave also shapes the type of person we become.

In contrast to values, ethics can be described as more prescriptive and deal with what is *right and correct* (Loewenberg and Dolgoff, 1992, p21). Whereas values can be described as beliefs or principles about what can be regarded as 'good' or worthy in social work, ethics represent the actions or behaviours which promote these fundamental beliefs. In other words, ethics represent guidelines about how social workers can translate their professional values into actions, and as a result, tend to be more prescriptive since they represent guidelines about how we ought to behave. In professional practice, since ethics deal with questions about 'what is right and correct', then it is the guidelines, principles and rules of conduct, expressed in ethical theories and codes of conduct, which seek to promote ethical practice. Ethical practice can therefore be described as the 'putting into action' of the values or principles that are attributed to professional social work.

While it is important to define these terms, it can still be difficult to separate out the two. I will try therefore to refer to ethics as representing ethical theories or principles codified in codes of ethics, since they are concerned with behaviour or action, but remind you that ethics are underpinned by core principles or values. Ethical practice in social work should represent a congruence between professional values and your practice. Since values are the primary determinant of our behaviour, we will now turn to consider the question of personal values and professional values in social work.

Personal values and thinking critically

The differences between personal and professional values are rather like the distinction between made in Chapter 2 between informal and formal theories in social work. Professional values can be said to represent the formal values of social work, written down and expressed as those values which should guide practice and typically tend to be those codified in codes of ethics or codes of practice. Personal values, as the name suggests, are those values which can be described as more informal and internalised. They represent what we as individuals think to be important and of value and in terms of guiding our behaviour, they may be less explicit precisely because we take them so much for granted as being 'good' or worthwhile ways of behaving. However, when looked at more closely, 'personal' values may in fact reveal themselves to be less personal (i.e. individual) than we might at first think, since they can often reveal themselves to be 'common' or shared values. Such values tend to arise from the society around us, stemming from the process of socialisation begun most often in our families of origin and reinforced through the education system and significantly reinforced through the influence of the mass media. However, significant social differences within our society, such as age, gender, socio-economic status, ethnicity and physical abilities, also result in considerable differences in life experiences which result in greater opportunities for differences in expression around 'common' values, or even a rejection of these values. Together, this can create differences and conflicts in attitudes. Such differences may make us less able to see commonalities in beliefs and attitudes and inadvertently reinforce the idea that personal values are more situated within the individual rather than socially constructed and which can cut across those social divisions identified earlier.

However, becoming a professional social worker requires you to think critically about your personal values and consider how they influence your practice. It is not simply enough to say that personal values have no place in professional social work, since our values are part of what makes us who we are and may, as suggested, be more collectively shared. The critical question, as DuBois and Miley (1999, p141) ask, is whether *personal values create barriers* in our practice. If we are too involved with our own values and seek to impose them on the service user, we are less likely to acknowledge the service user's views and wants, and equally, if we overidentify with the service user's values, then we may miss both subtle and important differences in their circumstances. Critical thinking requires us to think carefully about the values that we hold and their influence, since they shape our social world and, by implication, can influence our behaviour in our professional setting. Since we are working in a professional context, ethical practice requires us to think critically about how our behaviour, particularly in relation to service users, can promote good or positive outcomes for those we are working with, or at least that our professional behaviour minimises the potential for harm. The following activity invites you to think about some of the values which are important to you, thinking about their source of influence before asking you to consider which values you identify as important in social work.

ACTIVITY 3.1

(If you can, when you have completed this activity, try to discuss your answers with another student/practitioner who has also completed the exercise.)

1. List some of the values that you consider to be important to you. Would you describe these as 'common' or shared values, or more personally individual to you?
2. What are the significant sources of influence that have shaped your values?
3. What values do you think are important in professional social work practice?

Comment

As you have worked through these questions, your answers have revealed part of your value system and what you consider to be important. They are therefore part of what shapes you and informs your identity. Particularly in question 1, comparing your answers with others may reveal a propensity towards 'common' values, maybe such as the importance of family life, or the need to protect children from harm. However, of course, the potential for conflict lies in the prevalence of different views as to, in these circumstances, what constitutes a 'family' or what we mean by 'family life' and what is meant by 'protection' and 'harm'.

In terms of constructing your identity, in question 2, you may have identified more formal belief systems, such as religious or political views which have influenced your beliefs about what are important and appropriate ways to behave. Sometimes it may feel easier to express more formal or commonly shared beliefs, since others share their 'value' as well. This is not to suggest that such beliefs are beyond criticism, but because they are shared, there is some solace in the knowledge that one's political or religious beliefs are not just 'personal' but are shared by others. In other circumstances, personal values may be less formalised and seem more personal or intrinsic to us, and may reveal significant life events or experiences which have impacted on us and shaped our identify, such as the experience of family breakdown, or the death of a loved one. Such experiences (and of course you may have identified more positive experiences) reveal themselves as significant events that have impacted on you and influenced your perception or understanding of events and when 'un-picked' reveal your value biases. Such experiences may influence who we choose to work with as well as the focus of the work we undertake with service users. Without the process of 'un-picking' or critical thinking and analysis, it can be more difficult to discern an identifiable belief system as we may just feel that we are exercising our choice about who we choose to work with. Indeed personal preferences may be more positively expressed by identifying who you prefer to work with rather than not. Nevertheless, such choices can still reveal value biases and if expressed more 'negatively', such as social work with older people is less satisfying compared to work with children, can leave you vulnerable to criticism. As a result, you may choose not to reveal either oppositional views or to state categorically your disapproval or disdain for particular client groups or behaviours. This may reveal a concern to protect yourself from personal criticism or maybe even a realisation that such views are unacceptable in social work. The frequently cited social work value of being 'non-judgemental' has perhaps a lot to answer for, in helping to perpetuate the myth that social workers should be value-free in their practice. As Beckett and Maynard (2005) conclude:

> it is impossible to eliminate those personal values from professional decision-making. It is possible, though, to keep our values and assumptions under review, and be open to other ideas. And it is possible too to recognise that certain preferences or beliefs are irrelevant to the task in hand and should be disregarded. (p17)

In the next two sections we look at the professional context of social work and those values which are considered central to professional practice and you can compare the values identified with those you considered important in your answer to question 3 of Activity 3.1.

Professional context of social work

The professional values of social work shape what we can and cannot do in our work. This means that in our role as professional social workers we cannot just rely on personal values. Instead, there are expectations about how we ought to behave (that is, ethical considerations) which are influenced and guided by professional values that emphasise what is 'good and desirable'. This raises important questions about accountability and being able to justify our behaviour and the decision-making process in our work.

Professional accountability is about being able to account for our practice and this involves a process of explaining and justifying our actions. It means *that as social workers we are prepared to be open to the scrutiny of others for our actions, be prepared to accept praise and blame in equal measure and be prepared to explain our actions* (Parrott, 2006, p70). Traditionally, professional accountability has focused on a professional's need to be accountable to their clients or service users, emphasising that the professional must be *prepared to account for their actions to people using their services* (Banks, 2006, p2). However, within the context of contemporary social work practice, Banks (2006) stresses the importance of 'multiple accountabilities', which include being accountable to:

- services users
- carers
- employers
- outside agencies
- the public
- the legal system.

These considerations point to the potential for conflict in the social worker's role, which are demonstrated in Figure 3.1.

Figure 3.1 highlights the range of different demands that social workers can face in their role and the potential for conflict between these different areas. So it is not just that there are multiple accountabilities for us to be aware of, but there is also the potential for conflict between these that require, at best, a resolution, or at least skills in negotiation that enable us to work purposively in our role as a social workers. Beckett and Maynard (2005) suggest that behaving as a professional involves more than just the use of skills, competencies or being conscientious. It is about:

- *playing the role that you signed up to when you joined the profession, and*
- *setting aside your own personal feelings when they conflict with that role. (p73)*

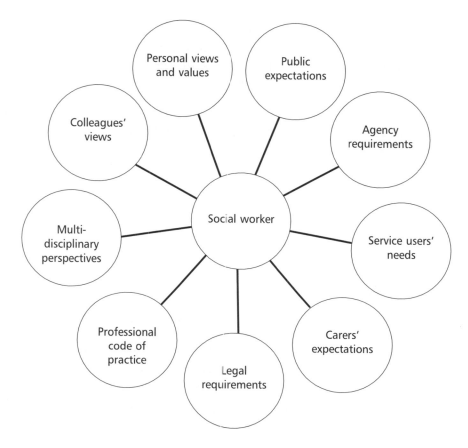

Figure 3.1.Competing demands for social workers

Banks (2006) develops this view but suggests that personal and professional values cannot be entirely separated, stressing the importance of the worker as a morally responsible agent. Banks proposes an integrative approach to considering the relationship between personal, professional and agency values. This can be seen as a three-part process, beginning with:

- *the person with their own moral code (who takes);*

- *the role of the professional worker (with professional values and codes of ethics) (who takes);*

- *the job of social worker (in a particular agency with specific responsibilities and duties). (p136)*

All three elements are influenced and circumscribed by societal norms, public opinion and the law and draw attention again to the approach of social constructionism that highlights social work as a changeable activity and the importance of critical thinking.

Banks' approach highlights the centrality of the individual acting as a moral agent (i.e. having values and acting ethically) who considers the compatibility and congruence between their personal beliefs and the expectations of their public role. It seems to me that Banks is emphasising the integrity of the worker, and that it is not just what a professional does that marks out a worker as behaving ethically, but that they think critically about what they are doing and the type of person they want to be. This is suggestive of an approach to ethical thinking based on virtue ethics, discussed later in this chapter. This seems a more helpful approach than the implication of Beckett and Maynard's suggestion that setting aside one's personal feelings when they are in conflict with our professional role, is unproblematic for the individual when faced with this decision. When we consider these points and the potential for conflict arising from the different demands highlighted in Figure 3.1, we are starting to engage in questions about ethical practice – that is, questions about the way we ought to behave and what is right and correct and the values that underpin professional practice.

Professional values–traditional values

A number of writers identify a continuation of 'traditional' social work values alongside the development of more 'emancipatory' values (Banks, 2006; Dominelli, 2002; Thompson, 2005). These traditional values build upon the work of Biestek (1961), an American Catholic priest, while the emancipatory values are attributed to the development of radical approaches to social work, dating back to the 1970s.

Traditional values tend to focus on the importance of the service user/social worker relationship and a number of core values can be identified.

- Respect for the individual as a self-determining being. Thus we treat service users as people of worth, regardless of our feelings towards them, or their behaviour, and equally, we treat them as having the freedom and ability to make decisions and exercise choice.

- Acceptance, which follows from the above. People are seen as unique individuals with particular needs rather than categorised or stereotyped according to their circumstances.

- Non-judgementalism. We should avoid judging the individual as undeserving or disapprove of them. Thompson (2005) sees this as making a 'moral judgement' about an individual's character or worth.

- Confidentiality. This refers to the service user being able to speak honestly with the worker without the concern that this information becomes freely available. Breaking this trust would inherently undermine 'respecting the individual'. However, the service user's right in this respect is not absolute and involves a consideration of agency requirements and the rights of other individuals.

Can you identify any limitations of the traditional values in contemporary social work practice?

Comment

You may have identified others, but a significant criticism with traditional values is their focus on the individual service user and the relationship with the social worker, which fails to take account of the wider context of contemporary practice, as highlighted in Figure 3.1. Equally, the focus on the individual minimises collective considerations and that many difficulties presented to social workers are not simply individual concerns but are situationally based, that is, they occur between individuals and couples and within families, as well as representing community difficulties or social problems.

Professional values–emancipatory values

Acknowledging the multiple accountabilities which social workers face and that many individual problems can also represent social concerns, Thompson (2005) suggests that traditional values have been 'transcended', that is, built upon to include 'emancipatory' or 'anti-oppressive' values (Parrott, 2006) which include the values of empowerment, partnership, minimal intervention and social justice. For Banks (2006) this approach is essentially *a moral–political stance...embedded in the commitment to working for social change* (p38).

Emancipatory values include the following.

- Social justice, which is perhaps an over-arching value since it lays the foundation for a commitment towards emancipatory ideals. Social workers deal with service users who are predominantly vulnerable, disadvantaged or marginalised and an understanding of these characteristics has increasingly been informed by a structural analysis of service users' circumstances, rather than just an individual focus (as discussed in Chapter 2). Indeed, as Thompson (2005) suggests, to work alongside these service users without a consideration of how these social inequalities impact on their lives, would represent unethical practice.

The value of social justice therefore includes a commitment to addressing and tackling these injustices experienced by service users and therefore supports the pursuit of greater social equality. Social justice:

> *embraces equality in all its senses of equal treatment, access to services and equality of outcome...[it] is based on the idea of distributing resources in society according to need...challenging existing power structures and oppressive institutions and actions.* (Banks, 2006, p39)

- Partnership. If we are committed to tackling issues of injustice which affect service users and thus to supporting greater social equality, it follows that an important principle, or belief which informs our work, should be partnership and working collaboratively with service users. This involves engaging and involving them throughout the assessment process, seeking out their views and valuing their contribution as equal participants in the process. Such a principle also extends to our working relationships with other colleagues as part of a multi-disciplinary approach to supporting and working effectively with service users.

- Empowerment. Like most of the values identified, this is a widely used term, with competing views about its meaning. Put simply, it is a process of service users gaining a sense of control over their circumstances, but used in a social justice context, has a more 'radical' meaning: *supporting and encouraging people or groups to realise their own power and take action for themselves* (Banks, 2006, p120), and draws upon the development of personal, interpersonal and political power to allow individuals or groups to improve their circumstances. Parrott (2006) extends this by emphasising two central components of empowerment. It is about *control – so that people define their own situation and their needs with this*, and secondly, it is concerned with *self-actualisation – enabling service users to then take power for themselves through developing their confidence and self-esteem, their skills and knowledge* (p38). (See Chapter 5 for a fuller discussion on empowerment and practising from an emancipatory perspective.)

- Minimal intervention. Parrott (2006) defines this as a value which is based on the recognition of the power differentials that exist between professionals and service users, and is concerned to allow service users early access to services to prevent their disempowerment.

Remembering Thompson's (2005) view that emancipatory values build upon traditional values, we can see how they reinforce each other. For instance, the traditional value of respect for the person as a self-determining being is not just limited to an individual focus, but links to the value of social justice which acknowledges the common characteristics which shape many service users' lives, just as empowerment supports the view of people as 'self-determining beings' able to exercise choice and control. Equally, acceptance or non-judgementalism must be an intrinsic part of an emancipatory approach, otherwise we are perpetuating discriminatory and oppressive practice and cannot work in partnership with service users, since we would be unable to acknowledge and work with their views. Finally, confidentiality should be an acceptable standard for any professional to hold. After all, we would not want our private information to be the source of gossip, either in work or in private. However, we know that confidentiality includes several caveats that include organisational responsibilities and protection from harm. Therefore service users and carers need to understand when information needs to be shared with others, and assumes the values of respect and partnership.

Professional codes of conduct

Expectations about professional conduct are best exemplified in codes of ethics or codes of practice which set standards of behaviour which the professional is expected to adhere to. In Britain, a code of ethics has been developed for social workers by the British Association of Social Workers (BASW, 2002), which is a professional organisation for social workers where membership is voluntary. In contrast, the British regulatory body for social care workers (which includes social workers) requires all social work students and social work practitioners to be registered with their country's social care council. Britain's four councils are state-funded organisations that are concerned with regulation, registration and matters of professional misconduct for social care workers, as well as the regulation of social work education and training. In England, the social care council is represented by the General Social Care Council (GSCC), which was established in 2001. In addition, the GSCC provides a code of practice for employers and employees, recognition perhaps, that in Britain, social work is largely practised within organisations rather than an individual private activity. Both codes can therefore be considered as *political counters constructed as much to serve as public evidence of professional intentions* [as to providing] *actual behavioural guidelines for practitioners* (Wilding, 1982, cited in Banks, 2006, p81). We will now look at the BASW Code of Ethics for Social Work before comparing it to the GSCC Code of Practice for Social Care Workers.

BASW Code of Ethics for Social Work

The BASW Code of Ethics is a 16-page document for guiding social work practice. It begins with setting out the scope and objectives of the Code, that is, *to express the values and principles which are integral to social work, and to give guidance on ethical practice* (BASW, 2002, p1) before providing a definition of social work. It then identifies the values and principles which social work is committed to. These are outlined below.

> *Social work is committed to five basic values:*
>
> *Human dignity and worth*
> *Social justice*
> *Service to humanity*
> *Integrity*
> *Competence*
>
> *Social work practice should both promote respect for human dignity and pursue social justice, through service to humanity, integrity and competence.*

The Code then goes on to discuss these five individual values in more detail, describing these as 'principles' under which social workers have a 'duty' to adhere to (section 3, 'Values and principles', of the BASW Code). Section 4 of the Code details 'ethical practice' providing guidance, but *not intended to be exhaustive or to constitute detailed prescription* (BASW, 2002, p7). Four specific areas of ethical practice are identified:

- responsibilities to service users;
- responsibilities to the profession;
- responsibilities in the workplace;
- responsibilities in particular roles.

The Code of Ethics fulfils a number of different functions. First, it serves to maintain professional status and identity, since it is concerned with how the professional sees themselves as well as how the outside world sees social workers; and secondly, it is concerned with guiding professional practice. However, inevitably the Code avoids being overly prescriptive, since this would run the risk of the Code becoming a kind of 'rule book' reducing social work practice to merely a technical rational activity. Instead Banks (2006) suggests the Code is most useful in detailing *the broad principles of the profession and the potential areas where ethical issues will arise* (p99). You can view the full BASW Code of Ethics on their website, www.basw.co.uk.

GSCC Code of Practice for Social Care Workers

In certain respects, the Code of Practice has a similar function to the BASW Code of Ethics, since it serves as a public document detailing the standards of behaviour that can be expected from social care workers and their employers. In addition, the Council acts as a regulatory body for professional practice with statutory powers to discipline and remove individual members from the register for professional misconduct and malpractice. However, it is a mandatory requirement that social worker students and qualified practitioners (included in the generic term 'social care workers') are registered with the Council, whereas membership of the BASW is voluntary. It could be argued that due to its legal authority over the BASW Code, some may see the BASW Code as increasingly irrelevant, but I will come back to this point later in the chapter. The GSCC outlines six *standards of conduct* that *social care workers are required to take account of* (GSCC, 2002). These are outlined below.

Social care workers must:

- *protect the rights and promote the interests of service users and carers;*
- *strive to establish and maintain the trust and confidence of service users and carers;*
- *promote the independence of service users while protecting them as far as possible from danger or harm;*

- *respect the rights of service users while seeking to ensure that their behaviour does not harm themselves or other people;*

- *uphold public trust and confidence in social care services;*

- *be accountable for the quality of their work and take responsibility for maintaining and improving their knowledge and skills.*

The Code then goes on to give more specific guidance about what is included in each of these six standards. You can view the GSCC Code of Practice on their website, www.gscc.org.uk.

ACTIVITY 3.4

Look at a copy of the BASW Code and the GSCC Code and compare them with each other. Consider the following three points.

- *Can you identify any limitations to the GSCC's preference for grouping social care workers and social workers together as a homogenous group?*

- *Does it make any difference naming the GSCC Code a Code of Practice rather than a Code of Conduct?*

- *Since membership of BASW is voluntary and registration with the GSCC mandatory, what argument would you make in favour of the BASW Code being just as legitimate and important for social workers to adhere to?*

Comment

In answering these questions, the following points should also be noted.

- Statutory social workers and social care workers perform very different roles and one significant difference is the legal authority social workers have to intervene in people's lives, which is not the case for social care workers. The first four statements of the GSCC Code are concerned with protecting service users, which Banks (2006, p99) suggests *should be obvious anyway*...[instead] *it is the more subtle and detailed use of power and knowledge* which social workers rely on which requires an ethical consideration of their behaviour and role. The conflation of social workers with care workers makes this more problematic.

- Since the GSCC Code refers to 'social care workers', it is broader in scope than the BASW Code and therefore not specifically related to 'social work' practice. The GSCC Code represents a more 'general' expectation of behaviour and runs the risk of being less concerned with 'ethical' behaviour, since 'general' expectations of behaviour represent general 'preferences' rather than prescriptions about the way we ought to behave (the definition of ethics adopted in this book). The general preferences of the GSCC Code may inadvertently undermine a consideration of the ethical dimensions of social work practice.

- Consequently, by omitting such terms as 'values' and 'ethics' from the GSCC Code, the Code may reduce a practitioner's willingness to consider the ethical dimensions of their behaviour and role, presenting practice as a rational and impartial activity, when clearly this is often not the case.

- This is further reinforced by the Code's preference for the term 'practice' rather than 'conduct'. The latter implies a consideration of behaviour, particularly its moral aspect and emphasises the responsibility we have to think about how we behave in our role, whereas the term 'practice' can serve to distance moral considerations from our behaviour, presenting social work as simply a practical activity devoid of its contentious nature.

- The GSCC Code of Practice does have more authority than the BASW Code of Ethics as a result of the former's regulatory function and role. However, in contrast to the BASW Code, there is no principled definition of social work, with a commitment to think about what we do. Instead social workers are now grouped under the generic heading of 'social care workers' who are located in organisations (also bound by a GSCC Code of Practice for Employers) whose role is to support them as frontline workers in carrying out their work, which includes the *use of legislation, practice standards and employers' policies and procedures* (GSCC, 2002). By locating the primary focus of attention on the practice of the worker, the Codes of Practice may unwittingly only serve to reinforce the division between thinking and doing, that is, between theory and practice. Viewed from this perspective, social work, subsumed under social care, becomes merely the act of doing where 'good' practice is concerned with completing and adhering to agency procedures. In comparison, the BASW Code of Ethics reminds us that 'good' practice in social work is premised on principled beliefs which should guide our practice as we interact with service users and carers. This view emphasises ethical conduct in social work as a conscientious activity that involves thinking critically about what we do and its effect on the service user and the nature of our role. One of the ways of maintaining our criticality is through professional education and training.

Critical analysis summary

Swindell and Watson (2007) point out the importance of developing effective and innovative teaching strategies to enhance the interest and motivation of student social workers in the development of ethical practice, particularly in relation to their professional codes of ethics. In their research, the authors adopt the term 'ethical delegate' to describe someone able *to see ethics as something they are, not merely as something they are required to follow according to educational and professional policy.* Creative or innovative approaches to teaching are those which move away from conventional 'I teach–you listen' approaches, or those that rely on the use of hypothetical case studies, which have the effect of distancing the student from an applied resolution of the ethical issue.

Comment

The increasing 'bureaucratisation' of social work (discussed in Chapter 4) has meant that agencies are increasingly drawing up codes of practice which emphasise the agency's responsibilities alongside service users' entitlements. However, these are not in themselves a substitute for ethical practice which is grounded in a consideration of the context and purpose of social work, and these are ethical questions. The BASW Code of Ethics recognises the 'practical–moral' activity of social work and the need for an ethical worker. The danger is that this may get overlooked if we just confine ourselves to a 'practical' consideration of the social work role.

Parrott (2006) suggests an 'intermediate' approach to understanding social work ethics, which sees professional ethics, that is, professional behaviour, as having to meet expectations of public morality as well as being in tension with it. This means that social workers are accountable due to their public role but equally, there are times when professional actions run contrary to public expectations.

> *This is turn requires a different set of ethics which can navigate a way between professional responsibility and community accountability. This intermediate position is not an easy one to maintain but it does adequately describe the often ambiguous position that social workers find themselves in when assessing the validity of societal values in their practice.* (p6)

The intermediate approach suggests that due to social work's mediating role, we cannot just rely on 'public' or commonly shared values to inform our practice. We require a professional code of ethics which acknowledges the potential for conflict that lies within contemporary practice, as well as an awareness of ethical decision-making processes which allow us to keep in mind the needs of service users, who, due to their vulnerable and disadvantaged situations, require ethical considerations in terms of supporting them to manage their lives more effectively.

We will return to look at ethical decision-making after we have considered the ethical theories which are drawn upon to help us determine ethical behaviour.

Ethical theories

Since ethics are underpinned by fundamental values or principles, there should be a congruence between our professional values and the way we behave in our professional role. We can therefore understand 'ethics' not just as professional 'codes' or prescriptions about the way we ought to behave, but also as representing coherent systems of thinking or theories about what is right and correct. In this section, we look at three main systems of thinking, or ethical theories which typically underpin beliefs about how social workers ought to behave.

To begin with, however, consider the following activity.

ACTIVITY **3.5**

You are on placement in an Adult Services team and are doing a home visit to Mrs James who has requested a community care assessment. At the end of the visit, Mrs James is insistent that she wishes to pay you personally £50.00 as a thank you for your help and time. You explain that you cannot take the money, and Mrs James reluctantly accepts your decision.

What reason/s would you give for not taking the money?

Comment

I hope that you would agree that taking the money would be wrong, but in your explanation, you may have drawn upon some of the reasons below.

- Accepting the money would be contrary to your duties as a social worker. You may still see the act of taking money as dishonest, but you focus more on your duties as a social worker and your professional relationship towards Mrs James. The professional relationship between the social worker and the service user means that it is always wrong to accept money from service users as it undermines public trust in your professional role.

- Taking the money would lay the foundations for expecting all service users to pay for social work services directly. If we took this money from Mrs James, then why not expect all service users to pay us personally for our services? Here you are concerned about the potential harmful consequences of accepting money from service users who cannot afford to pay and therefore view the act of taking money as wrong because it can lead to unfair outcomes.

- Taking the money would mean you were acting dishonestly and being exploitative. Service users do not pay directly for social work support and therefore we should not take money for our own personal gain.

All three explanations rely on different ethical theories to explain their justification that accepting money, for our personal use, directly from service users for our professional services is wrong. We will now consider the basis of these three different ethical theories.

A deontological approach

A deontological approach emphasises the importance of duty or rights in the decision-making process. From this view we therefore have a moral duty to behave in a particular way based on a principled belief or obligation, regardless of the consequences. Such an approach stresses the importance of 'absolute' or 'fixed' principles which guide our behaviour. Their definitive nature emphasises the importance of consistency and universalism in the decision-making process. (It is important to add that moral duties are not the same as legal duties or obligations. A legal duty or obligation requires the worker to act according to a legal requirement, but the worker may not feel that this is a moral obligation.)

The most influential deontological approach is based on the work of the German philosopher, Immanuel Kant (1724–1804). In social work, a key principle based on Kantian ethics is that of 'respect for persons as a self-determining being' and that individuals should not be used or treated as 'a means to an end' but rather, that individuals have intrinsic value simply because they are human and therefore we should not value people because of their perceived usefulness. A Kantian-derived approach to ethical thinking and behaviour stresses the importance of rational thought and reasoning in the decision-making process and acting from a sense of duty, rather than inclination. In social work, the importance or primacy of the relationship between the worker and service user is stressed alongside the worker's sense of duty to that person.

In Activity 3.5 regarding Mrs James, the first explanation adopts a deontological approach to the morality of not accepting the sum of money. This view emphasises the social worker's duty towards the service user and not using her as a means to an end and only valuing her in terms of the financial benefit to the worker. Instead, you emphasise the importance of respecting and valuing Mrs James. Using another example, you may hold the view that social workers have an obligation or duty to support and work with service users in an anti-oppressive way, adopting principles derived from an emancipatory approach. This may bring you into conflict with your agency or colleagues, but you may feel this is a moral duty or responsibility which guides and informs your practice. Your practice is guided by these principles, regardless of consequences.

However, a deontological approach may well involve competing conflicts of duties or rights between, say, a service user and his or her carer, or between a conflicting duty to be mindful of costs and the rights of a service user to an expensive treatment or service. A deontological perspective therefore does not prevent us from having to think about the consequences of our decision-making, but rather, that this is not our primary focus.

Utilitarian consequentialism

This second approach draws upon the English philosopher, Jeremy Bentham (1748–1832) and its later refinements by his student, John Stuart Mill (1806–73). Consequentialism draws upon the principle that the morality of an action is determined by whether its outcome is *favourable or unfavourable* (Beckett and Maynard, 2005, p39). Such an approach immediately raises the question of which principles determine an action to be favourable or unfavourable.

In social work, the wider dimensions of practice also impact on our role, and increasingly we need to see beyond our relationship with the individual service user, and must also be aware of the legal and procedural dimensions of our practice, our responsibilities to our employing agency, as well as being mindful of resource costs and the need to promote public welfare. In adopting a consequentialist approach, Banks (2006) suggests two important principles which should inform our decision-making.

- the principle of utility, which is concerned to promote 'the greatest good for the greatest number';

- the principle of justice, which is concerned with distributing services as widely and/or fairly as possible.

In the example of Mrs James, the second explanation adopts a utilitarian consequentialism approach since the social worker is concerned that if the principle were established of accepting payment from service users, then we would expect all service users to make personal payments to social workers. This argument draws upon the principle of 'rule utilitarianism' which relies on *general rules of conduct* (Beckett and Maynard, 2005, p39) that are judged according to the principle of utility. Accepting payment, therefore would lead to the general expectation that this was acceptable and expected from all service users, but yet this undermines the principle of justice, since it fails to acknowledge a service user's ability to pay and therefore represents an unfavourable outcome against those who cannot pay for services. For the social worker in this example, accepting the money is wrong because it is ultimately unfair and disadvantages poorer service users.

Although the principles of utility and justice are important in social work, we can see that they may also conflict with one another. For instance, the principle of utility favours a majority approach, since it is concerned with promoting the greatest benefit for the greatest number of people, but this can undermine the principle of justice and its concern with distributing services according to need. If we favour utility principles over principles of justice, then we uphold the needs of the majority over the needs of minorities and undermine a key principle of emancipatory social work and the BASW value of 'social justice'.

While utilitarian consequentialism can offer us a framework for guiding us in moral decision-making, it is not *founded on one ultimate principle that can be used to decide all conflicts between other principles, rules or alternative courses of action* (Banks, 2006, p37).

Combining principle-based ethical theories

Both a Kantian-derived ethical theory and a utilitarian approach provide a framework of principles for helping us to determine the 'right and correct' way to behave. However, they are both equally formulaic, with the former relying on principles of duty or obligation which are absolute and should be applied universally. The utilitarian approach requires us to consider principles of utility and justice in weighing up the likely consequences of whether our actions result in favourable or unfavourable outcomes for the majority of recipients. Yet the complexity of contemporary social work practice means that often we are faced with conflicting or competing demands and requirements from different stakeholders, such as those between a service user and their carer, or between the needs of an individual resident compared with the rest of the group members, or requirements to utilise resources 'most effectively'. Banks, (2006, p48–51) therefore proposes a combined set of Kantian, utilitarian and radical approaches which draws upon three principles, or fundamental beliefs which set the standards for ethical behaviour in social work. These are:

- dignity and worth, which stresses the importance of treating people as ends in themselves, regardless of who they are or what they have done, or indeed their capacity;

- welfare or well-being, which includes both individual welfare and social welfare;

- social justice, which embraces the concepts of equality and justice and is concerned to promote equal treatment, equal opportunity and equality of result – in addition, distributive justice is also embedded in the principle of social justice and is concerned with distributing goods according to certain rules and criteria.

None of these three principles takes precedence over another and neither do they prevent conflict among them, but as Banks (2006) remarks, in social work (and indeed in many professions) *principle-based approaches have tended to dominate professional ethics* (p51) but in social work, these three principles lie at the heart of social work practice. They therefore require not only a critical understanding of their meaning, but from the social worker, require qualities of *confidence, commitment, motivation and skills to put these principles into practice in difficult and challenging contexts* (p52). This calls to mind a third ethical theory which is gaining increasing popularity in the literature on social work ethics.

Virtue or character-based ethics

In contrast to Kantian or utilitarian-derived approaches, which focus almost entirely on the actions which a person performs, virtue or character-based ethics focus on helping people to develop good character and motives. The emphasis on the former approaches shifts from one which focuses on the question of 'which action should I choose?' to one which asks 'what sort of person should I be?' The focus in virtue ethics is on the person's motive as the defining feature of their morality, not their action, as in Kantian-derived or consequentialist ethical theories. Virtue ethics thus provide a powerful corrective to the tendency in ethical decision-making to focus on duties or rules, or the calculated outcome, as the defining principle for determining actions that allow a person to decide how to behave in any particular situation. Instead virtue ethics shift attention to a consideration of what makes a person 'good' by considering their behaviour in terms of motive rather than outcome.

For McBeath and Webb (2002), principle-based ethics are the antithesis of a morally grounded social work. *Kantian and utilitarian ethics to a degree rely, respectively, upon the mechanical application of a right-claim and adherence to duties, or upon the comparison of anticipated outcomes'* (p1018). The dominance of rule-based and duty-based ethical perspectives is perhaps unsurprising, given the context of contemporary social work practice with its reliance on policies and procedures resulting in increasingly standardised practice (Jones, 2001; Jordan, 2001; Stepney, 2000). In virtue ethics, however, it is the worker who is viewed as the site of moral integrity, not their actions. From this approach, we should be less concerned with questions about 'what is good social work?' and more concerned with questions of 'what is a good social worker?' since it is the moral conduct of the worker that is the key concern.

From a virtues perspective, it is the intention of the worker that is most important – it is not that they follow rules or act from a sense of duty to do the right thing, or that they are able to predict the favourable outcomes of their actions, but rather, that they place themselves as an active participant in moral decision-making processes and engage in questions about the type of worker they think constitutes a 'good' social worker.

In the example of Mrs James, the third explanation represents a virtue approach. The worker stresses the importance of personal qualities which are important in the relationship between a social worker and the service user. In this case, the qualities of honesty and non-exploitation are emphasised. The morality of the decision does not rest on defining the act of accepting money as intrinsically wrong because it conflicts with the worker's sense of duty or a concern over unfavourable consequences. Instead what is most important is that it is the social worker herself who becomes dishonest by accepting the money, and this is not a quality that she defines as part of being a 'good' social worker. Thinking about the qualities that you consider important in a social worker, encourages you to be reflective about your behaviour and whether this can be defined as the actions of a 'good' or 'bad' social worker. This reinforces accountability as more than just action and 'public' accounting about our practice, but that we also have a moral responsibility to think about the type of worker we value and want to be like, and that we need to be accountable to ourselves as well.

Virtue ethics also draw upon the importance of the particular relationships we have with each other and in professional social work, these relationships are based on the cultivation of professional values to inform our practice and our behaviour. Parrott (2006) draws upon the work of Clark (2006) and identifies five qualities that are appropriate for professional social work:

- *Commitment to learn new skills.*
- *Commitment to social justice.*
- *Enabling.*
- *Morally inclusive.*
- *Competent in social situations.* (p57)

McBeath and Webb (2002) emphasise the virtues of *judgement, experience, understanding and reflection and disposition,* (p1016) as important qualities to cultivate in our relationships with service users in order to help us make sense of what is going on and inform our decision-making. For the social worker committed to the development of virtue ethics, the pursuit of a 'good life' involves an understanding of the relationship between views about the nature of society and the role of the social worker and this involves the cultivation of certain virtues in our character which we use in our interactions with service users. We judge the situation, using knowledge, skills and virtues and act according to the situation we find ourselves in. Since it is our virtues that drive us to do the best we can do in any particular situation, we are always striving for best practice according to the needs of the service user and in pursuit of the well-being of society (McBeath and Webb, 2002).

When we remind ourselves about the ends to which we act, which professionally should be based upon our view about the purpose of social work and therefore our role, the professional relationship between social worker and the service user (be it an individual or the community) becomes more central and we become more mindful of the values we hold and how we feel we ought to behave. However, immediately we start thinking about our values and questions about how we ought to behave towards people, we face a dilemma: how do we behave towards service users when we have to deal with aspects of their behaviour which we might object to, for instance, offending or physical violence, or when we are working with service users we do not like – we do not 'click' with? Are virtue and character-based ethics enough to ensure that the service user still receives an equitable service? While these approaches are important and remind us that ethical decision-making is not just about the outcome of an action but affect the person carrying out the action as well, we need to remember that virtues are also culturally determined and in many cases situationally dependent as well, and therefore a reliance on virtue ethics can still result in conflicts of opinion about ethical behaviour and decision-making. It is likely therefore that ethical practice will draw on a plurality of approaches which include duty-based and consequential considerations to inform our approach to practice and decision-making.

Banks (2006) goes on to argue that while virtue ethics provide an important corrective to the tendency to blindly adopt a rule-based approach to decision-making, in fact rules and principles are particularly important, precisely because we do not always behave in a virtuous way, despite the expectation that professional activity should entail consistent behaviour. Such a concern makes us mindful of the potential for harm or abuse in the social work relationship (and hence the centrality of the relationship in social work) and thus rules and procedures do offer some protection against dishonest or abusive behaviour. However, an overreliance on such rules can easily result in defensive and mechanistic work practices that detract from a concern about ethical issues which pervade the world of the social work.

Components of ethical decision-making

In this final section, we look at the components of ethical decision-making based upon the work of Cassuto Rothman (1998). She describes ethics as *a discipline based on thinking* (p10) which includes the ability to understand, reason and reflect clearly and logically about the issue. Thus, fundamental to an ability to engage in ethical decision-making is the prerequisite that one is able to exercise free will or has the ability to make choices. As Rothman suggests, if we are unable to choose between meaningful alternatives, then ethical decisions are not possible. In addition to having a choice, you must also be able to put these choices into effect, or act upon them. Ethical decision-making is therefore a process of reasoned thinking where there are choices available as to what to do, and further, that such choices are capable of being put into action. Given that social work is characterised by work with vulnerable and marginalised groups and people whose lifestyles or personal difficulties bring them into contact with statutory social services, we can see again how central a consideration of ethical issues is to social work practice. The value of partnership means that service users are increasingly expected to engage in the decision-making process involved in their situation. The value of 'respect' also means that we need to be sensitive to people's differential ability, such as when working with people who may be confused or experiencing severe mental ill health; those with a mental or developmental impairment; or children and young people who may be unaware of or feel ambivalent about the ways they are expected to behave. Such individuals may have a limited ability to participate in a decision-making process, and of course, there are those individuals who may feel so vulnerable or marginalised that they feel incapable of exercising choice and engaging in shared decision-making. The ethical element of social work therefore is not just that we tread an awkward line between society and the individual, but more so, that we are frequently in positions of power compared with our service users. The decisions and choices that they are faced with may seem obvious or inconsequential to us, but can often represent a difficult process for the service user to engage in. The danger lies in making decisions on others' behalf without due consideration of their effects on the individual concerned.

Rothman (1998) therefore suggests four components of ethical decision-making which involve:

- defining the ethical problem (what the matter is);

- gathering information relevant to the problem (meaning-making);

- determining an appropriate theoretical base, then exploring professional values, understanding the service user's values, and recognising the impact of the worker's personal values;

- weighing up options and reaching an accountable decision.

We can see that the components of ethical decision-making are not dissimilar to the assessment process – an interpretative process that forms a core skill in all aspects of social work. An assessment refers to the systematic gathering of information for the purpose of making sense of the case material. It is both a cognitive and analytic process whereby the practitioner seeks out the meaning of the case before deciding which method of intervention is most appropriate. As Parker and Bradley (2007) state, *Assessment is part of a continual process which links with planning, intervening and reviewing social work with service users* (p8).

Since assessments are a dynamic process it is not always possible to discern discrete stages, although Meyer and Palleja (1995) identify four key stages of an assessment that have parallels to Rothman's ethical decision-making process. The first stage begins with 'exploration' and letting the service user tell their story. Meyer and Palleja (1995) suggest that:

> *the most effective way of learning about a client is by understanding his or her narrative (however it is related), helping to organize it, and hence making sense of past events that are affecting the presenting problem.* (p117)

Although in many instances, the service user is the primary source of information, social workers may also draw on other sources of information and other agencies to help in this process. The exploration stage concerns itself with determing whether there is a case or not – the social worker and service user are in the process of determining 'what the matter is'. This process parallels Rothman's first stage of ethical decision-making, that is, being able to define the ethical problem.

Meyer and Palleja (1995) refer to the second stage as the 'assessment phase', where *the practitioner uses his or her knowledge and judgment to interpret or make sense of the story* (p119). In 'making sense', we are in the process of meaning-making and draw upon our professionally acquired knowledge and research, say about child development or mental health, in order to help us understand the difficulties being experienced. Our professionally accumulated knowledge and experience are what help us to do our job. The perspectives that we draw upon to make sense of the social world include our personal and professional values and frame our understanding of what we think the matter is. Drawing on our skills of critical thinking and reflection directs us to particular kinds of knowledge and practice methodologies in order to intervene most appropriately. The assessment phase is concluded with 'problem definition' or perhaps less problem-orientated, 'selecting a focus'. Ethical practice assumes the service user's preference always plays a vital role in determining what the matter is and what is to be worked on.

When we know what the matter is, we can focus and plan our intervention strategy (the third stage of the assessment process). This draws on our knowledge base and consideration of what works and best practice ideals and *must take into account the resources that are available in the community and in the client's life* (p121).

The second and third stages of the assessment mirror the same stages of Rothman's ethical decision-making process, but since both processes are interpretative, we need to remember not to think of them as discrete stages, but rather, that we are in the process of trying to make sense and meaning-making, drawing upon the range of skills and knowledge that we possess, as we try to work towards a consensus of the issues involved in the situation that has arisen.

The final stage of the assessment process is 'termination' or ending and offers the opportunity for review. Given its inevitability, endings in all our work should always be kept in mind, even from the beginning, so that both the practitioner and the service user can focus on the outcome of the work together.

Assessments provide a means of making explicit our choice of intervention and therefore make our work available to scrutiny and have the effect of increasing accountability and effectiveness in our practice. In considering the ethical issues prevalent in a case we can see that the assessment process can also help identify the ethical dimensions to our practice. The process of determining 'what the matter is' in the exploration stage and 'meaning-making' may well reveal ethical considerations which influence how we relate to our service user or the focus of our intervention. Although ethical issues pervade the social work task, we may not see or acknowledge an ethical dimension to our work, but that does not negate its presence. Since the assessment process is key to any area of social work practice, and has parallels with Rothman's ethical decision-making process, alongside a consideration of ethical theories and professional values and expectations about how to behave, the critically reflective practitioner should be able to maintain an ethical focus in their practice and allow for service user involvement in the process. The interpretative nature of both processes means that we have to maintain a critical perspective about the sources of knowledge we draw upon to inform our practice and the ethical decisions we make.

We can also draw on Swindell and Watson's (2007) critical analysis of developing ethical practice (identified earlier in the chapter), and the importance of developing effective learning techniques to identify ethical dilemmas that arise in practice. A simple but effective learning technique is the consideration of ethical dilemmas identified by students while on placement. Students work in small groups and discuss their placement, drawing out ethical issues they have experienced, and consider how ethical theories and codes of practice enable them to make better sense and how their shared understandings enable them to contribute towards an ethical resolution. The following case study (based upon a student's real practice experience) identifies one such example and the group's working through of a resolution.

CASE STUDY

The service user is an 89-year-old man, who lives alone and has been diagnosed with moderate dementia. His daughter is 71 years old and visits him throughout the day to provide him with meals, help him dress and attend to his personal care needs. The man has two sons who visit weekly but are not involved in providing personal care. The daughter has requested her father be placed in long-term residential care due to his care needs and deteriorating mental health, and this request is also supported by the family doctor who feels the daughter's emotional and physical health is deteriorating due to the demands of caring for her father. The two sons do not want their father to move into residential care and believe his care needs can best be met at home, with the daughter's continued support and the provision of domiciliary care by a care agency. The father remains unaware of his daughter's request or the conflict of opinion between his children and the family doctor. However, when prompted, he admits that he wishes to remain at home with the support of his daughter.

The dilemma identified in this example is the conflict between the daughter's needs and wishes and those of her father, as well as the opposing views of the sons and their wishes. However, the group identified several other important conflicting factors:

- *the service user remains unaware of his daughter's request and this represents a threat to his autonomy;*

- *the daughter's perception of her father's needs conflicts with his wishes;*

- *the doctor's view of the service user's health care needs conflicts with his patient's health care needs, i.e. the daughter;*

- *does the daughter have the right to decide her father's future?*

- *should the daughter continue to look after her father?*

The group recognised the need to work as part of a multi-disciplinary team, i.e. with the family doctor as well as with all the family members; however, the difficulty they identified was how to work towards a positive resolution that acknowledged everyone as having a legitimate viewpoint. In working towards a resolution, the group identified the role of the GSCC Code of Practice and its emphasis on both service user and carer as equally important, but they also looked towards formal ethical theories in helping them make sense and reach an understanding, and identified the following.

- *Deontological principles of respecting autonomy and how this impacted on both daughter and father as both deserving the right to personal autonomy. This led the group to establishing a moral principle that it was the right thing to do to inform the father that a request for residential care had been made by his daughter, and that this was supported by the family doctor, who acknowledged both their different health care needs.*

- *The sons' reliance on a deontological principle that their father had a right to remain in his own home and the emphasis on family duty to support this.*

- *The principle of utility and the role of the social worker to seek a resolution that supported a majority viewpoint, but also a consideration of the consequences for the daughter that her continued role as a carer was threatening her own welfare (and this view reinforced the importance of the father being party to the decision-making process).*

- *The use of a virtue-based approach by the group that supported the view that resolution was only possible by being reflective about their own personal view that 'it was the right thing to do' to allow the father to be party to the decision-making process and that his deteriorating mental health was not an excuse to exclude him from discussions and that he was still worthy of inclusion in the discussions about his future.*

- *This virtue approach reinforced the group's view about social work as part of reflexive-therapeutic approach that drew upon the social worker's skills and knowledge in mediating with all those concerned and allowing them to express their feelings openly and appreciate their different 'standpoints', but also the commitment to working towards a positive resolution, which acknowledged the consequences of the family's decision-making.*

CASE STUDY *continued*

- *This 'talking approach' demonstrated a pluralistic approach to ethical decision-making, which drew on different ethical theories, a knowledge of the GSCC Code as well as the process of being reflective about their practice that enabled the group to acknowledge their personal views as well and an awareness of their view about the nature of social work.*

Once the family were enabled to talk openly and to involve their father in the decision-making process, several packages of care were identified but in the end, the father felt, now that he was aware of his daughter's view and her needs, that residential care would be the most suitable option of care for him. This approach enabled the family to maintain a positive relationship with each other and support their father in his move to residential care.

C H A P T E R   S U M M A R Y

In this chapter we have explored the centrality of values and ethics in the decision-making process and highlighted how much our professional practice is mediated by questions of values and how we should behave. Professional codes of ethics and practice have an important role to play therefore in terms of helping to formalise our beliefs and highlighting ways in which we are expected to behave. In order to understand the principles which inform these codes of conduct we have also looked at three main ethical theories which impact on social work; namely, duty-based and consequentialist theories and virtue-based approaches. The first two ethical theories are often described as principle-based theories and are action orientated, since ethical concerns are worked out through the application of guiding principles and focus on determining ethical action. In contrast, virtue ethics concern themselves with questions about what makes a person 'good'. Actions are not considered right regardless of motive. Although principle-based approaches remain dominant in teaching about ethical decision-making and in professional codes of conduct, this does not deny the importance of relationship-based or virtue ethics. Such approaches remind us of the importance of personal qualities that we might wish to find in a social worker as well as emphasising a particular approach to social work that should be more than the acquisition of technical competencies. By locating the site of moral integrity within the worker, virtue ethics have a particular resonance with the approach taken in this book – we should not just be concerned with how to make moral choices but should also engage in questions about the morality of our work and how we make moral decisions and the processes by which our moral attitudes develop. Our professional education and practice training are vital in beginning this process of critically examining our attitudes and beliefs about the nature of society and the role of social work, and questions about how we relate to our service users and how this informs the decision-making process. The emphasis shifts from merely a focus on 'what should I do?' to one which also asks 'what kind of a person should I be?' It is more difficult to hide behind the screen of technical rationality and action-based principles when we put ourselves forward as the critical site of responsibility.

FURTHER READING

Bowles, W, Collingridge, M, Curry, S and Valentine, B (2006) *Ethical practice in social work.* Buckingham: Open University Press.
An accessible text which builds upon your understanding of ethical decision-making and problem-solving through the application of case studies.

Parrott, L (2006) *Values and ethics in social work practice.* Exeter: Learning Matters.
Provides good coverage of how ethical considerations pervade the practice of social work.

www.basw.org.uk The website for the British Association of Social Workers. This will allow you to review their Code of Ethics and it is also a useful and informative site, providing national and international news and events about social work as well as education and resource material.

www.gscc.org.uk The website for the General Social Care Council, the English regulatory body for social care workers. This provides information about news and events, details about training and learning in social work and post-qualifying courses, and will also allow you to review their Codes of Practice for Social Care Workers and Employers.

Chapter 4
Social work and its organisational context

3.1.5 **The nature of social work practice.**
- The factors and processes that facilitate effective inter-disciplinary, inter-professional and inter-agency collaboration and partnership.
- The processes of reflection and evaluation, including familiarity with the range of approaches for evaluating welfare outcomes, and their significance for the development of practice and the practitioner.

3.2.4 **Skills in working with others.**
Develop effective helping relationships and partnerships with other individuals, groups and organisations that facilitate change.

Introduction

Compared with more traditional professions, such as law or medicine, there are few opportunities for social workers in Britain to practise independently of an organisation. Although there are opportunities for independent practice and consultancy work, it is likely that the practitioner will be contracted by an organisation to undertake the required work, and therefore, the organisation remains a dominant medium of practice. Therefore, social work can be described as almost exclusively a corporate activity. It is not only that social work takes place in, and is guided by, organisational constraints, but we also guide our service users through organisations in order to support and respond to their assessed needs. So, at times of physical or mental ill health, terminal illness or complications or problems at birth, social workers can be involved or liaising with other organisations, such as hospitals, the Department for Work and Pensions, or with schools. Part of our role will be guiding people through these organisations and, in turn, organisations influence our practice, in terms of meeting the requirements of the organisation as well as legitimatising and sanctioning our actions by virtue of the statutory duties and policies which social workers are charged with. So, it is only in our professional capacity, acting for an agency, that we carry out investigative interviews or undertake an assessment for services for a person requiring support. In other words, it is the organisational site that manages the roles and tasks which social workers must carry out. In addition, these agencies control many of the resources required by workers to work with service users. Ultimately therefore, social work organisations represent a major source of social work power, as sites of statutory duties and gatekeepers to resources.

This chapter looks at social work in its organisational context and considers the role of the agency and how it shapes contemporary practice. By the end of the chapter you should be able to:

- understand and define a social work organisation and the distinction between formal and informal structures;

- identify the changing and contemporary organisational context for social work;

- define what is meant by the term 'managerialism' and its impact on contemporary practice;

- consider the role and importance of supervision and the importance of reflective practice in shaping and informing your practice.

Defining a social work organisation

What is meant by a social work organisation? Firstly, drawing on the work of Robins (1990), Mullender and Perrott (2002, p75) describe an organisation as *a consciously co-ordinated entity, with a relatively identifiable boundary, that functions on a relatively continuous basis to achieve a common goal or goals.* Similarly, Hafford-Letchfield (2006, p4) draws attention to the importance of an organisation's function and purpose and cites the work of Buchanan et al. (2004), who describe an organisation as *a social arrangement for achieving controlled performance in pursuit of collective goals.*

In considering these definitions, the importance of understanding how organisations can impact on your practice should be noted. In particular, it is your practice that helps contribute towards the function and purpose of your organisation. The description above, of an organisation as *a social arrangement*, draws attention to the fact that organisations are not self-functioning – they exist by virtue of the people who work in them and therefore it is important to understand their formal as well as informal structures and consider the issue of organisational culture as influencing its performance. The idea that an organisation also exists for *achieving controlled performance* draws our attention to the importance of management and how these *social arrangements* are managed in pursuit of the agency's aims or goals.

Increasingly, social work agencies or organisations are referred to as part of *the human services* (Thompson, 2000) and refer to:

> *a range of occupations sharing the common theme of dealing with personal and social problems. This includes nursing and health care generally; social work and social care; youth and community work; probation and community justice; counselling, advocacy and mediation.*

These occupations are typically part of a formal group of organisations whose aim is to enhance *the social, emotional, physical and/or intellectual well-being of some component of the population* (cited in Hanson, 1995, p207). As part of a network of welfare services, human services organisations share two key characteristics:

- *Their raw materials are people who become clients and are transformed or changed in some specified manner.*

- *They are mandated by society to serve the interests of their client as well as those of society.*

(Hanson, 1995, p207)

We know social work agencies are created to address particular social concerns or problems and therefore social work is a socially mandated activity, designed to carry out certain roles and functions. These responsibilities are subject to competing definitions and expectations, as we have seen in earlier chapters. However, practice is not just something that happens 'out there' with service users and carers, but also pens within the organisation, where conflicts of interest or expectations be' colleagues, people who use services and with managers, can also affect how the organisation is managed internally and how we 'manage' our own workload.

Managing the 'process of social work' therefore is not just something that is done externally, through government policy and legislation, or internally through a super-vision process, and neither is it just social work practice with service users. Instead, all these things involve a process of management, and therefore the concept of 'manage-ment' is central to the practice of social work.

Social work and management

Payne (2002, p226) describes the process of management as comprising three levels represented by:

- personal management;
- people and organisational management;
- strategic management.

If we begin with personal management and move up these levels, the degree of organisational management increases. Personal management is something which we all do, more or less. We have to manage our workload, and prioritise through a process of decision-making, our time and the tasks we undertake. These are skills that we take with us in all areas of life, not just in the workplace. As the name suggests, personal management is a skill involved in organising ourselves. In the context of social work, it is the process by which we, as practitioners, manage our working day and is the reason why Coulshed and Mullender (2006, p13) suggest *all social workers are managers* drawing on skills which are equally managerial.

ACTIVITY 4.1

Write down any practitioner skills that you can identify which you think are transferable to a managerial context.

Comment

Like Coulshed and Mullender (2006, p14), you may have identified the importance of people management skills and the need to engage in *purposeful interpersonal rela-tionships* as central to both the practitioner and manager. In addition, the practitioner relies on the key skill of assessment – a multi-dimensional process that draws on the importance of clear communication skills, such as listening and hearing, as well as written and verbal abilities; observational skills; decision-making and problem-solving skills; liaising and working with other professionals in developing services that respond to assessed need; managing and negotiating the process of change; working collaboratively with service users and other professionals; and the ability to review and evaluate your intervention. These are some of the key skills practitioners are required to develop and utilise in both direct work with people who use services and they are also transferable skills required in a managerial role.

Returning to Payne's (2002) work, this second level of management, people and organisational management, typically refers to managers of frontline staff, team leaders or managers, or aptly named resource managers. These are people whom Payne (2002) refers to as *middle management,* mainly involved in organising other people and resources. These managers will therefore inevitably impact on our personal management, as they will come with organisational expectations as well as carrying with them their own view of personal management.

At the top level, strategic management is represented by senior managers, whose job will entail the development and implementation of organisational and public policy and the strategic management of the service, in terms of both physical and human resources. We can see that these levels are not independent of each other, but interact. In managing our time, for instance, at the personal level, we are deciding how to prioritise and allocate our time in terms of carrying out our roles and responsibilities as part of our conditions of employment. However, in working with colleagues, other professionals and service users, we are also operating at the second level (people and organisational management) and in our role as a social worker, we obviously negotiate policies and procedures and that makes us aware of the strategic influence of management.

All three levels therefore represent different sorts of management activity and are tied into the roles and functions of the organisation at a formal level and at an informal level in terms of how they are understood and interpreted.

Formal structure of a social work organisation

Traditionally, understanding the formal structure of an organisation has drawn upon a rational or scientific focus on structure. Such an approach is best exemplified by the German sociological theorist, Weber (1864–1920). Weber identified such formal organisations by their emphasis on bureaucratic administrative structures, supported by hierarchical authority structures and a division of labour with specialised task arrangements in pursuance of specific organisationally defined goals that drew upon 'rational–legal authority' to run the organisation. We can therefore recognise the formal structure of an organisation as represented by its stated goals, written rules and policies and procedures which guide employees' routine actions. These procedures and legislation are designed to ensure the operation of the organisation as well as govern practice activities. The Codes of Practice set by Britain's Social Care Councils also impose an obligation on employing agencies to ensure that social care workers are able to carry out their legal requirements to at least minimum standards. In addition, formal structures are characterised by a division of labour necessary to carry out the function of a social work agency, for example, the team clerk, receptionist, social worker and team manager. We are introduced to the formal structure of a social work agency through placement experiences, inductions and mission statements and staff manuals detailing operational expectations, as well as having an awareness of where we 'fit' into the organisation by virtue of our job title and role. Thus a team clerk would not expect to be involved in the decision-making process at a strategic management level, any more than a manager at this level would expect to accompany a social worker on a duty child protection initial investigation visit. As an organisational form, this traditional rational hierarchical model *focuses on management as a way of structuring organisations and the tasks they undertake, controlling the people within them so that the objectives of the organisation are met* (Payne, 2002, p228).

It is this type of organisational structure which has most typically dominated the practice of social work, whether practice is expressed within large local authority social services departments or within voluntary organisations. In such places, *a high value is placed on personal and organisational accountability... conformity comes from following formalised rules and procedures and working within clear-cut structures* (Coulshed and Mullender, 2006, p29). Furthermore, it is the post, not the individual, that carries the specific responsibilities, for which the individual occupying it should have the relevant skills.

Two main advantages can be identified that relate to this type of model.

- Firstly, the emphasis on hierarchy and predictable rules and procedures means that workers and people using the service, have a clear idea about lines of command and what they can expect, thus increasing opportunities for accountable practice.

- Secondly, for workers, career opportunities are based upon the acquisition of appropriate skills to fit the job description, where the emphasis on 'rational–legal authority' means that rules are expected to be applied without favour.

However, in a social work context, such a model also attracts criticism, summarised by the work of Coulshed and Mullender (2006) in the summary below.

- The emphasis on *routine, stable, unchanging tasks* remains problematic for social work practice due to its contingent nature and emphasis on unpredictability and change. In practice, therefore, this can result in routinised practice that remains unresponsive to individual need.

- Heavily bureaucratised organisations can curtail the practice of social workers who are expected to exercise their professional judgement and practise largely autonomously in their work with service users. Social workers are expected to *make specialised, individualised and complex judgements about people and their lives... the hallmark of the qualified profession.* Instead, the term *bureau-professionalism* may be more appropriate for social work practice.

- A hierarchical and rule-bound organisation can result in a rigid, unresponsive approach to stakeholders, such as workers themselves, service users and carers, employers, professional and regulatory bodies and partnership agencies, who make competing demands on the organisation.

- The increasing diversification within health and social care provision and the growing need for 'partnership working' between such organisations is resulting in ever more complex organisational structures, cutting across operational line management structures, with:

  an increasing need for non-social work, technical specialists to manage or advise on whole parts of the organisation or department's activities, such as computing, legal or equalities issues [which can] cut across operational line management, that is, across the overseeing of the basic business of that department or agency.

  (Taken from Coulshed and Mullender, 2006, pp31–3)

Increasingly, therefore, it is recognised that this formal, rational presentation of an organisation masks the multi-dimensional and complex reality of how organisations actually operate. While there is no doubt that social work organisations can be experienced by workers and service users as rigidly structured and highly formalised, alternative perspectives exist that also attempt to explain how organisations operate.

Human relations management is one such approach and:

proposes that relationships between people carrying out tasks within the organisation are crucial to the success with which objectives are met. It emphasises aspects of the organisation such as 'culture', the collective identity of members of the organisation and formal and informal groups within it.

(Payne, 2002, p229)

This view of an organisation represents the 'human' aspect of an organisation and as an alternative model of an organisational structure, provides a better means of understanding the contemporary complexity of managing the practice of social work. We shall return to this after we have looked at the impact of modernisation and managerialism in social work, and how a human relations perspective can help navigate around the changing realities of social work practice.

Modernisation and managerialism and its impact on social work practice

We have seen in Chapter 2 the increasing influence of the individual rights and responsibilities discourse which was constructed by the British Conservative government from the late 1970s. This dominant discourse marked a shift away from a collective welfare consensus which favoured state-funded welfare provision as the best means of meeting people's welfare needs. At this time also, the dominant organisational structure for managing the tasks of social work were primarily located in local authority social services departments, which, we have seen, tended to adopt a traditional bureaucratic structure for managing and administering social services.

The individual rights and responsibilities discourse favours the view that the individual, not the state, should take primary responsibility for managing their welfare, either through self-sufficiency or relying on the private or voluntary sector, with state services acting as a safety net for those most vulnerable or unable to meet their needs, or those unwilling to take responsibility for themselves. Under the Conservative government, statutory social services came to be used as part of a mechanism for dealing with problems of *social polarisation, exclusion, poverty and disadvantage rather than part of a strategy for preventing them* (Jordan, 2000, p140).

The welfare changes initiated by the Conservative government were also embraced by the New Labour government of 1997, and social work's role as a force of containment rather than alleviation continued. Local authority social work become increasingly concerned with the surveillance of high-risk work and the completion of comprehensive assessment documentation with the therapeutic interpersonal work, traditionally associated with the role of the local authority social worker, increasingly passed over to the independent and voluntary agencies (Jordan, 2000).

Under the banner of modernisation, New Labour continued to reduce the role of the state in welfare provision, instead favouring an increase in state involvement in terms of regulation and evaluation of services. Public services continued to be criticised as sites of inefficiency and ineffectiveness and being unable to recognise the need for progressive change. In terms of the impact on social work practice, it was the publication of *Modernising social services* (Department of Health, 1998) which laid the groundwork for many of the organisational and practice changes that have since become the contemporary landscape of British social work.

The main policy initiatives of the modernisation agenda are summarised below.

The modernisation agenda reflects an overall emphasis on service regulation in order to raise standards, drawing on:

- performance indicators and league tables, providing information to a range of different stakeholders;

- an emphasis on 'best-value' and effective practice models;

- partnership working and co-ordination between different welfare professionals and their organisations;

- increasing service user participation;

- greater public accountability;

- registration and discipline of social care workers and continuous professional development.

All these initiatives have led to dramatic changes in the organisation and management of social services and social work practice. In particular, the *pull of partnership* (Lymbery, 2007, p180) and the emphasis on increasing service user involvement and participation in the services they require have resulted in a split between adult and children's services. Changes in children's services were initiated following the inquiry into the death of Victoria Climbié and the subsequent review of services that followed.

In particular, Lymbery (2007, p180) identifies a number of concerns that were high-lighted:

- *The lack of co-ordination of agencies involved in child protection.*

- *Failures of collaboration and problems in respect of management and accountability.*

- *Individual practitioner weaknesses.*

The development of separate children's services is intended to improve inter-professional collaboration and co-ordination of services and encourage higher levels of professional accountability within the services. For social work practitioners working in this field, they can no longer assume that the organisation they are working in supports a unique social work focus. Compared to their traditional 'homeland' of local authority social services departments where line managers were most likely to have been drawn from the ranks of social work practitioner, these new organisations are concerned with delivering holistic services and meeting performance indicators, with managers who may well be drawn from different professional backgrounds. The change in organisational goals may also reflect a move away from a traditional social work focus. For instance, the creation of Youth Offending Teams, while adopting a multi-disciplinary approach, may reflect a more punitive approach based on 'just deserts' and criminal justice. This is in contrast to the more traditional approach of social work based on reform or rehabilitation, focusing on the development of more socially acceptable interpersonal skills and factors that promote resilience.

In adult services, the development of separate services has been more concerned with developing principles of user participation and inclusion in the control of their services (Hudson, 2005). This has resulted in an increasing convergence of health and social care services in the field of adult services. Although at first sight, this might appear a compatible merger, there still exists potential for conflict in terms of social work practice. For instance, Healy (2005, p20) highlights:

> the biomedical discourse [as] one of the most powerful discourses shaping practice contexts, particularly in health services, such as hospitals, rehabilitation services and mental health services…[It] is also influential in a wide range of social service contexts, such as child protection practice where medical experts often play a pivotal role in defining and assessing what counts as evidence of risk of harm and abuse.

This means that even in multi-disciplinary teams, such as mental health or learning disabilities, where joint working has been in existence for several years, a biomedical perspective is likely to dominate the practice context, thereby undermining a psycho-social approach which is the hallmark of a social work focus. In addition, Lymbery (2007) highlights what he terms the 'duel' between health and social services over budgetary responsibilities, with the former organisations becoming more successful in the fight to transfer these responsibilities, thereby relieving the pressure on their budgets.

In addition to changes in organisational structure, performance indicators have become a significant force in the drive to modernise social services. This has resulted in the development of a set of national standards and indicators which social services are expected to achieve, to be used as part of a nationally collated set of publishable data detailing their performance in identified areas. For the first time, this has *provided a public statement of targets for social work and social services and a mechanism for measuring how well councils [are] doing – in effect, the first ever nationally established framework for describing and evaluating the effectiveness of social work* (Coulshed and Mullender, 2006, p65). While there is no doubt about the importance of social work remaining a purposeful activity with clear aims about its involvement, this criterion has nearly always been applied on an individual basis between worker and service user, rather than tied to organisational and national target indicators. There is the potential danger, therefore, that practice may become skewed towards meeting these performance targets and a situation where predetermined and measurable outcomes become more important than process. This is a concern that has long been expressed in the social work literature, where social work has been identified as subject to increasingly tighter and more prescriptive practice requirements. While the modernisation policy initiatives 'talk the talk' of social work, emphasising partnership and inclusion and assessment based upon need, how social workers carry out their duties and responsibilities is increasingly experienced by workers as a practice which is highly regulated, characterised by rigid procedures and a commitment to outcome measures and *aggressive* managerialism (Jones, 2001). Such a practice effectively militates against face-to-face client contact and lays the foundation for highly routinised work. Such an approach to practice is known as managerialism and reveals itself in a practice which emphasises *technical recording, systematic information gathering [and] performance indicators ...[all of which] tend to reinforce mechanistic practice rather than creativity and innovation* (Stepney, 2000, p12). Taken together, they effectively curtail professional autonomy and reduce much statutory social work to a rational technical activity (Adams, 2002). In the field of adult community care, Stepney (2000) identifies care management as more of a policy initiative aimed at cost containment rather than quality and is one that is at odds with the values of delivering needs-led, empowering services. Likewise, Jones' (2001) research with frontline workers identifies their concerns that management attempts to control budgets had driven out the welfare ideals seen to lie at the heart of social work practice.

Jones' research on social workers' views about their work represents a damning indictment of contemporary practice – *the job is awful* (Jones, 2001, p551) – but it is the context in which they practise that is identified as the cause – the clients, those people who are consistently identified as the most vulnerable and disadvantaged in our society, were seen as having reasonable, if not only modest demands for services. However, the context in which social workers operated was identified as preventing them from offering a service that could make a difference to the quality of their clients' lives. The impact of managerialism and the contract culture was seen to have resulted in a complex web of procedures and bureaucracy severely curtailing social workers' abilities to carry out creative work with clients which, for so many, symbolised their *raison d'être* in the profession.

Although the practice context of social work is argued to be dominated by an emphasis on procedures and managerialism, historically, the educational context has also been seen to support this perspective of workforce regulation, reflecting the needs of employers. Orme (2000) charts this as a trend going back over 20 years, with reviews of social work training increasingly mirroring the needs of employers and an emphasis on a competency-based approach to practice and assessment. Although the current three-year undergraduate programme adopts the use of employment-led national occupational standards (NOS), occupational standards can remain concerned with attempts to measure observable behaviour and have attracted the same concerns that were elicited by the use of a competency-based framework (Adams, 2002).

A central concern about competency-based approaches to practice is that they can undermine process thinking and de-contextualise the service user's behaviour. Process thinking is part of the skill of critical analysis which is involved in thinking through the information you gather as part of a systematic approach to assessment in order to begin to make sense of the service user's situation. This is part of the qualities of professional judgement that emphasise critical understanding of the situation. You are therefore concerned that your assessment and intervention brings about a positive outcome for people who require your services which enables them to function or participate more effectively and goes beyond a short-term measure. Process thinking can be further understood by applying a psycho-social perspective to your assessment, that is, seeing and understanding the individual within their wider socio-economic context and how these factors may also impact on their situation. We thereby come to recognise the uniqueness of the individual as well as recognising commonalities of experience which may impact on individuals of similar backgrounds. The danger with a competency-based approach within a managerial context is that it can undermine this critically creative process. With the pressure of prescriptive assessment schedules and a focus on outcome measures, 'depth' explanations run the risk of being passed over in favour of quick fixes or short-term solutions. Service users become 'de-contextualised' in the concern to manage their behaviour rather than an attempt to understand their situation. In this way social work assumes an individual focus devoid of understanding wider social factors and commonalities of experience. Such an approach is the antithesis of critically reflective practice. Instead we need to look towards an educational context that acknowledges the risk and uncertainty of contemporary social work practice and supports a curriculum grounded in critical analysis of theory and practice. While social work might occupy an ambiguous position, social workers should be clear about their responsibility to service users and that it forms a key value requirement for social work practitioners and social work students under the national occupational standards as well as a requirement under their professional code of practice (see Chapter 3). Acknowledging the realities of social inequalities and the impact of material disadvantage on vulnerable and marginalised groups and individuals is a central component of anti-discriminatory practice (ADP) and is a practice principle that is well enshrined in social work education and practice and requires a critical appreciation of the context in which social workers operate.

Having looked at the impact of modernisation and managerialism in social work, take some time now to write down how you feel these two factors have impacted on the practice of social work and altered the organisational context in which social work has traditionally operated.

Comment

Hopefully, few commentators would argue with some of the key principles of modernisation, since they can be seen to represent aspects of good practice in social work, namely:

- increasing service user participation in the decision-making process and greater involvement in the control of services to meet their needs;

- use of performance indicators and targets aimed at improving efficiency and monitoring effectiveness;

- greater emphasis on professional accountability;

- partnership working and co-ordination between different welfare professionals and their organisations.

However, the challenges to social work practice should also be noted.

- Increasing convergence of health and social care organisations means that social workers can find themselves working in organisations that no longer have an explicit social work focus. This can result in conflict between different organisational priorities and professional identities that can manifest itself in poor team dynamics and low staff morale.

- League tables arising from performance indicators and target-setting can result in the threat of financial penalties for organisations, leading to an emphasis on work that can be easily monitored and processed, rewarding measurable outcomes at the expense of more in-depth and complex work which remains less susceptible to quantative measurement.

- These concerns have been expressed as a conflict between social work as a *technical–rational activity* rather than a *practical-moral activity* (Parrott, 2006; Payne, 2005) which emphasises the importance of critical reflection.

- Managerialism emphasises the role of the manager as a key driver in reforming services and increasing their efficiency. Its roots lay in the individual rights and responsibilities discourse and the application of market principles in the provision of welfare. While this might be the reality of contemporary welfare services, the critically reflective student and practitioner need to ensure that services are being delivered that still maintain the values of social work. There are alternative organisational structures that stress the importance of leadership and management and are more in line with social work's values. This is explored later in this chapter.

In the next section, we look at the influence of culture and informal structures which perhaps more acutely illustrates how organisations can be experienced by workers and people who require services.

Culture and informal structures

We know that organisations have a formal structure, particularly in terms of stated aims and purposes, as well as in the use of differentiated roles, for instance. The traditional rational view of an organisation would have us believe that these personnel perform their roles in almost totally predictable patterns, according to rules and procedures in pursuit of the organisation's aims, and that this is the means by which services are delivered. However, informal structures also exist within organisations, where structures are more fluid and more clearly linked to members' personal attributes. Informal structures can be revealed by observing who people talk to and where they go for advice and how they actually do their job in practice. This last comment alludes to the prevalence of 'practice wisdom' among practitioners. Practice wisdom reveals a familiarity with task or outlook which modifies the formal expectations of how, for instance, the task, should be completed. Agency cultures develop as part of the informal structure of the organisation. The workplace culture refers to *the learned and shared assumptions that regulate people's behaviour, such as communication styles and levels of cooperativeness* (Hanson, 1995, p210). Although workplace cultures reflect the values of the organisation at a formal level, they become reinterpreted at an informal level and may result in a disjuncture between the stated (formal) goals of an organisation and how it is actually experienced in practice. For instance, many social work agencies make explicit their commitment to equal opportunity policies or anti-discriminatory practice, but yet, at the point of entry, in their contact with reception staff, service users for example, may feel they have not been treated respectfully in a way which confirms a commitment to anti-discriminatory practice. However, this does not of course just pertain to service users. Since we bring 'ourselves' to the workplace, with our personal histories and identities, insecurities and our belief systems, workplaces are just as likely to reinforce dominant modes of behaviour and dominant social norms (Mullender and Perrott, 2002).

The following example demonstrates the pervasiveness of stereotypical assumptions which can influence how service users are treated or thought about.

CASE STUDY

A local child care agency operated a 'drop-in' service for parents who had child care concerns. One day a man called at the office wanting to see someone. The receptionist observed that he was a large, heavy built man, dressed casually in a vest top and jeans on a hot day. The receptionist asked him to wait while she contacted the worker. The receptionist explained to the worker that the man was in the waiting area, but she was worried about his appearance and feared he might become aggressive and asked the worker if she wanted someone else with her while she saw the man. However, the worker declined. The service user was not known to the agency and there was no evidence about his behaviour that suggested he might be aggressive. The receptionist's concerns were based on a value judgement about the man's appearance. As it happened, when the man spoke to the worker in private he become highly distressed that he could no longer see his children as he was separated from his wife, and she had now left the area. His wife had used the threat of legal action against him if he tried to pursue contact with his children and the man explained he felt inconsolable. In particular, he felt he had little choice but not to pursue this as he said he 'knew' how he looked to others. He described himself as 'a big bloke' and his wife was petite and his physical appearance often meant that people tended to assume that he was domineering and could be aggressive, but this was far from the truth. In fact, it was him who had sustained violence and aggression from his wife.

Such an example is a salutary reminder that formal rules and codes of conduct about behaviour are difficult to translate into a practice which remains objective and predictable towards all service users. Thus, there can be considerable differences in staff's daily activities compared with the agency's purported values as expressed in the formal documentation. An agency's culture will also be moulded by many factors, such as its history, its institutional and physical setting.

ACTIVITY 4.3

Before we consider how these three factors can impact on an organisation, take some time to consider your own experience of a human services organisation, and how the organisation's informal structure might be mediated by these three factors.

Comment

In Britain, for instance, given the long-standing association between charitable organisations and their philanthropic and religious roots, a child care voluntary agency may be influenced by its pioneering and reformist history, as well as its close association with Christian values. Its charitable status may also engender a belief among its workers and supporters that the organisation is involved in 'worthwhile' (or 'deserving'?) work. Such a belief may be further reinforced by the organisation's aim, stated perhaps in its emotive name, which may make explicit reference to its concerns about children's welfare. Voluntary organisations may also enjoy more public support for their agency compared with the more ambiguous relationship social services enjoys and this may create a culture of 'elitism' or 'specialism' in the workplace. Elitism can have a dual effect on its service users. Firstly, service users may believe they receive a higher-quality service from an organisation due to its specialist purpose, but in turn elitist attitudes can also pervade the assessment process and we know this can result in discriminatory practices towards service users. This last comment reminds us of the pervasive influence of 'culture' which influences staff interaction among themselves and service users and carers, as well as the communication networks that develop between the agency and other organisations.

Institutionally, workers may also feel their role and contribution more or less valued, depending on their agency setting. For instance, hospital social work can be described as 'social work in a secondary setting' and workers may struggle to have their professional opinions valued within a medical setting, despite the formal requirement and expectations for multi-disciplinary working.

Finally, the culture of an agency can also be influenced by its physical setting, for instance, a community children's resource for 'looked after' children, may have to work proactively with the local community to develop and maintain community support. Such active involvement may not be considered necessary for an area office located in a local council town hall, where a 'one stop' reception area may reduce the stigma attached to entering a specific social services agency.

Thus cultures develop over time as workers respond to the pressures of their job, establish support networks and create a work environment. Informal structures are therefore instrumental in oiling the wheels of an organisation (Hanson, 1995) and provide clues and explanations to the functioning of an organisation at a formal level. The human relations approach to working in organisations suggests that it is the relationships between people carrying out tasks within the organisation that are crucial to the success with which objectives are met (Payne, 2002).

Clearly the degree of access to the organisation's decision-making resources affects an agency's culture and contributes to a work environment in which staff and service users feel more or less valued. Invariably, this impacts on the work done, staff morale and ultimately, the service received by the organisation's service users.

RESEARCH SUMMARY

In Jones' (2001) research interviews with experienced social workers employed by local authority social services, he identifies their accounts of the growing stress faced by them as front-line state social workers, where a significant factor of induced stress reported by workers was the stress from above (p551) arising in part by the prevalence of poor and sometimes aggressive managerialism (p552) and by an increasing number of government and agency polices. They also spoke of their perception of endemic organisational change... driven by concerns to improve the quality of services but never involv(ing) any consultation with those who actually attempted to provide the services (p552).

Clearly, dealing with organisational change is partly dependent on context and, of course, the internal structures that exist, but the research is clear; fostering a positive change environment requires collaboration between the workers and those initiating the change (Bilson and Ross, 1999; Coulshed and Mullender, 2006; Pugh, 1993).

> *Effective leadership and management of change helps to develop a healthy organisational culture which involves service users, carers and the community through to employees, the management team as well as those who fund, contract with and have any interest in the organisation.*

(Hafford-Letchfield, 2006, p25)

So, for instance, the introduction of new procedures can be better supported through open dialogue between senior managers and team managers, with a clear rationale as to why change is considered appropriate. However, gaining the support of frontline workers is crucial, since very often they are the ones who will have to implement the change. A recognition of their role as 'operators' of the new procedures, alongside the seeking of their views, means that change is more likely to be on the basis of co-operation rather than conflict. Bilson and Ross (1999) suggest a change strategy based on systems principles deriving from the work of Gregory Bateson. They suggest that rather than trying to create change based on appeals to people's belief systems through rational argument only, change is encouraged in part through reflection and getting people to think about the consequences of their actions. Engaging people emotionally then allows the discussion to move in a more rational direction. Using systems approaches can help *to look for different ways of tackling difficult situations* (Bilson and Ross, 1999, p141). Creating a change environment requires opportunities for feedback (views of social workers, for instance) and the re-examination of the area of concern for change. This re-examination is also known as 'news of difference' as the re-examination can challenge belief systems. The challenge for successful change, however, is the *need to be open to adopting new and different understandings of the work* (p153).

It is important to remember that all agency members are stakeholders who share an interest in the success of an organisation and their place in the organisation. In turn, since all organisations are concerned to promote their own success, there is a need to *foster social work agencies as 'competent workplaces'* or learning organisations (Pottage and Evans, 1994, cited in Mullender and Perrott, 2002, p78).

Leadership and management

The focus on human relations as an aspect of management is part of a move away from the traditional hierarchical bureaucracies which have characterised statutory social services, presenting them as standardised systems of operation and service delivery. Instead, human relations management attempts to recognise the 'human' aspect of an organisation and that the quality and commitment of the staff are just as important as the management structures to a successful organisation. Such an approach has the potential to challenge what, for many workers in social services, has been an oppressive experience of managerialism. It is therefore part of a shift away from a functionalist analysis of the workplace to one which recognises that it is the human quality which has the potential to create and support practices aimed at improving service provision and design and encouraging greater participation and involvement of people who use services. This approach therefore lends itself to developing an emphasis on leadership as a crucial aspect of management. Like the focus on virtue ethics discussed in Chapter 3, the human relations approach emphasises the centrality of the person responsible, that is, the leader, rather than focusing just on the tasks required, i.e. management. The emphasis on leadership as a central component of effective management, looks to the qualities or characteristics of the person and is representative of the more personable term 'leadership'.

Looking back to Payne's (2002) typology of organisational structures, a clear purpose needs to be articulated throughout the whole of the organisation and at a strategic level, points to the importance of having an overall strategy which guides the organisation in terms of its aims.

> *The strategy must be supported by an operational plan or nothing will actually happen...[Strategic planning is therefore] about setting organisational objectives and then mobilising available resources [including financial, human and information resources] and the integrated activity of staff to achieve these objectives.*

> (Coulshed and Mullender, 2006, pp91–2)

An inherent characteristic of an organisation is change – organisations change internally as well as needing to respond to external factors. Government-initiated policies emphasise the importance of social care services providing services that promote more choice, independence, partnership and user control of services. This we know has resulted in different organisational structures and greater inter-professional collaboration between different organisations in order to meet these challenges. Together, this has implications for the way services are delivered and managed, making change a continuous reality. A successful organisation is therefore one that can take its workforce with it. Purposeful and strong leadership is crucial in helping to create adaptable workplaces capable of responding appropriately to the needs of their varied stakeholders.

In terms of management structures, this requires a working environment in which systems are flexible and adaptive, with clear lines of responsibilities alongside a strong sense of professional accountability so that the working environment remains responsive to different needs. There are several components to this.

- Such an environment implies a dynamic structure that cuts across and throughout the organisation.

- A sense of dynamism within an organisation supports accountable practice, where workers feel they can make a positive contribution towards influencing an organisation's goals.

- Organisational goals are twofold, in so far as goals can be externally driven; for instance, the need for performance indicators or targets and the translation of legislation and policies for effective practice, but human services organisations are also there to serve the interests of their service users, and this perhaps is the lynch-pin of effective leadership.

A good leader not only understands the function and purpose of their organisation and understands its 'business' but also recognises its 'people serving' function as well. So it is not just impersonal organisational or management accountability that matters, but the people who work in the organisation make it accountable to the people it serves: workers, partnership agencies and the people who require the service – service users and carers.

Strategic leadership therefore refers to those people who have:

> *prime responsibility for developing a language and organisational identify that binds everything and everyone together and inspiring them towards collective action and loyalty to the organisation's mission . . .* An effective leader seeks *to achieve a quality of life in the organisation that will generate and sustain commitment of the internal and external stakeholders to its goals.*

(Hafford-Letchfield, 2006, p25)

ACTIVITY **4.4**

Thinking about a human service organisation that you are familiar with, identify and write down what qualities or skills you think demonstrate effective leadership.

Comment

In terms of the qualities or skills that good leadership should aspire to, you might have drawn upon qualities such as:

- vision – a clear understanding of the agency's goals and mission and the ability to adapt to change and foresee possibilities;

- integrity – a sense of commitment and belief about the purpose and mission of the organisation;

- effective communication and a commitment to developing and sustaining partnership working in pursuit of delivering effective and responsive services;

- valuing the workforce – recognising the multiplicity of roles and function that go to make up an effective organisation and that 'people matter';

- fostering a 'learning environment' which supports and encourages individual learning in line with their personal and professional development;

- the ability to manage resources effectively and effective conflict resolution.

The value base of social care organisations

The Audit Commission Report (2004) identified the importance of a 'business-like' approach to managing social care services, one which was also underpinned by a strong emphasis on the values of social care and an understanding of why this is important. In other words, the values of social care emphasise the importance of a critical awareness of the impact of disadvantage and exclusion on people's lives. Organisations and leaders in human services therefore need to develop services that respond appropriately to people's needs and remain responsive to the value base of social care.

*Look back to the values of social work outlined in Chapter 3. Thinking about an orga-
nisation that you are familiar with, how far do you see these values reflected in the
management practices of your organisation?*

Comment

One way of beginning to think about this is to consider your role, as a student or
practitioner of social work, and the kind of work you do with service users, such as
assessment, planning, consultation and liaising with other professionals or service
providers, and reviewing and evaluating interventions, for instance. What type of
management practices support you most effectively in carrying out and developing
your role?

The *Leadership and management paper* published by Skills for Care (2006), identifies
what leadership and management practice should actively aspire to in social care.
They should:

- inspire staff;
- promote and meet service aims, objectives and goals;
- develop joint working/partnership that are purposeful;
- ensure equality for staff and service users driven from the top down;
- challenge discrimination and harassment in employment practice and service
  delivery;
- empower staff and service users to develop services people want;
- value people, recognise and actively develop potential;
- develop and maintain awareness and keep in touch with service users and staff;
- provide an environment and time in which to develop reflective practice, professional skills and the ability to make judgements in complex situations;
- take responsibility for the continuing professional development of self and others.

The values of social work are not just meant for the practice context when working
with service users and carers, but are part of the ethos of social care generally. We
would therefore expect to see them reflected in human services organisations and the
management structures that exist to drive the organisation, since the purpose of the
organisation is to meet the prescribed needs of service users. Human relations-inspired
management and leadership will therefore recognise the importance of workers as
well as formal structures in meeting these needs and that there should be a congruence between the two.

The values of social work require a critical appreciation of the social effects of disadvantage and marginalisation that shape the many people's lives who require the

support of social services. This calls to mind a critical understanding of social structures and how they can impact on and shape our lives, as well as an appreciation of psychological factors that gear our assessment and intervention towards person-centred planning and call upon a commitment to collaborative and partnership working. Practice and organisational structures therefore have to share a common value base to ensure purposeful practice in line with the purpose and goals of the organisation. Acknowledging and working towards this is not an unrealistic goal, but neither does it imply that this is not a difficult task. This is true of the view of social work practice which recognises it as a contested activity, characterised by competing views about its purpose and involving the management of risk and uncertainty. The nature of social work involves managing these tensions and conflicts and engaging in ethical decision-making that seeks the best possible resolution, even if this is not a perfect fit. An emphasis on virtue ethics and critical analysis calls to mind the kind of practitioner we want to be and that we will make judgements about others based on a critical appreciation of competing views and that in professional practice, we are all accountable for our actions. Leadership and management skills should be subject to the same kinds of critical analysis that we apply to our own practice and how far an organisation's structures support us in developing professional and accountable practice. Strong professional leadership and management structures are therefore essential in order to implement social care objectives.

Management and support of practice

For effective practice and responsive organisations, there needs to be congruence between professional practice and the goals of the organisation. One of the qualities identified for effective leadership was about valuing the workforce and developing their potential. This is required in order to promote organisational success and turns our attention to the concept of a 'learning organisation'. The Social Care Institute for Excellence (SCIE, 2004) identifies five key characteristics of a learning organisation, summarised below.

Summary of key characteristics of a learning organisation

Organisational structure

- Service user and carer feedback and participation are actively sought, valued and resourced, and used to influence and inform practice.

- Team working, learning and making the best use of all staff skills are integral to the organisation.

- There is cross-organisational and collaborative working.

Organisational culture

- There is a system of shared beliefs, values, goals and objectives.

- The development of new ideas and methods is encouraged.

- An open learning environment allows learning from mistakes and the opportunity to test out innovative practice.

- Messages from research and new evidence are thought about and incorporated into practice.

Information systems

- There are effective information systems, for both internal and external communication.

- Policies and procedures are meaningful and understood by everybody (based on a human rights and social justice approach).

Human resource practices

There is continuous development for all staff including a clear supervision and appraisal policy.

Leadership

- There is capacity for the organisation to change and develop services over and above day-to-day delivery.

- Leadership at all levels embodies and models the key principles of a learning organisation.

Focusing on workforce development and managing and supporting practice through formal supervision provides a key function in developing and supporting professional practice in social work.

The value of supervision

An organisational policy on supervision is vital to raising the profile of managing practice across various departments. Such a policy statement requires a recognition of the importance of all staff members' supervision needs and is not just restricted to students and practitioners of social workers.

ACTIVITY *4.6*

Look back to the case study earlier in this chapter with the receptionist, and consider what requirement for staff development would be useful for the receptionist.

Comment

In learning organisations there is a need to match the management of the organisation, or 'organisational maintenance', with a commitment to the management of practice across all staff members. An overreliance on organisational maintenance is likely to foster a restrictive managerial approach which favours rigid procedural practice at the expense of a reasoning process which lies at the heart of critical and reflective practice.

An organisational policy on supervision seeks to define supervision and its importance, as well as making clear its purpose. Supervision then becomes the mediator between the worker and the tasks of the organisation. It allows for the personal process of reflection and critical thinking about practice, but it also allows practice to be judged in line with the organisation's task of providing client-centred services. In the case study mentioned earlier, the receptionist could be encouraged to think about her 'common-sense' perceptions of service users and consider the usefulness of anti-discriminatory practice training in raising her awareness about stereotypical assumptions.

Monitoring and evaluation processes are also key in determining whether supervision results in an improved service. This requires that all those involved are clear about the importance of recording and the extent of confidentiality. This makes the supervision process open to scrutiny in terms of effectiveness, equity and organisational purpose. The focus then moves beyond just the needs of the worker, to a consideration of practice outcomes and their usefulness for people who use the services. This allows for the process of critical reflection about our practice and learning needs and also alerts the organisation to staff development needs, as well as highlighting areas of good practice. The quality assurance process, so often experienced as a 'top-down' process, has the potential in organisations that are responsive about the contribution of staff, to become a more reflective and reflexive process.

We can now begin to see the constituent parts of managing practice through supervision. Firstly, supervision represents a management function that is two-fold:

- it contributes to the management of the organisation in terms of aims and purposes;

- it contributes to the management of practice in terms of ensuring practice is 'client-centred'.

Secondly, supervision has an educative role, which allows time for thinking and reflection, a time to stop and pause and think about what we have done, to question practice and custom and an opportunity to consider if our practice is in danger of becoming routinised. Opportunities to question and critique our practice are vital to the development and support of effective practice. Inevitably, such reflections may also show up formal learning needs as well.

Finally, supervision should be a supportive process. The characteristic of social work as represented by risk, uncertainty and change as well as stress for the worker, cannot be overstated. This is part of the stuff of social work and social care, and workers need a supportive environment in which they can talk about the impact of their work. A well-integrated supervision process should be able to support as well as challenge the work practices that contribute towards stress and burnout, contributing to ineffective and poor practice, as well as staff ill-health. Organisational structures should therefore contribute towards the management and support of practice.

Jones et al. (2005) point out the importance of organisational context in terms of managing effective practice and suggest that *levels of readiness for change* is most high in organisations which are perceived by their employees as *strong in human relations value* (pp370–80). Following their review of the literature, Jones et al. (2005) conclude that the culture of a human relations organisation is *generally consistent with engagement, development and performance management capabilities* (p381). In other words, the organisation is more likely to have in place systems that help *facilitate individual and collective behaviour towards better change outcomes* (p381).

While there is an optimum organisational context and structure for helping to facilitate change and improve practice, the reflective practitioner also looks to themselves as a change agent and in the final section of this chapter, we look at developing the skills of the reflective practitioner.

The reflective practitioner

We have seen that the government-driven modernisation agenda has pushed social work into an activity that has generated criticism about its managerial focus. Regardless however of what view is taken about 'the nature of social work', one thing remains constant, and that is that social work has always sought to mediate between the individual and the wider community. Social work therefore remains a purposeful activity where we should be concerned to bring about a positive outcome for the service user, or at least avoid doing harm. Although the organisational context is an important part of promoting effective practice, as developing professionals we also have a responsibility to develop and support our practice development and the concept of the reflective practitioner emphasises our own role in developing and maintaining high standards of practice, as much as we can.

ACTIVITY 4.7

You should already have an idea about what is meant by reflection, so take a few minutes to complete the following activity.

● *How would you define the term 'reflection' and how can this process be used to aid your professional development?*

Comment

Reflection can be described as a process of *thinking about an experience or an event* that draws on the skills of enquiry and interrogation to identify why this particular event is important to you. It is a process that helps to make concrete our learning. Boud et al. (1993) describe reflection as a generic term to describe the process involved in exploring experience as a means to enhance our understanding. While reflection seeks to raise our awareness of an event or experience to inform our practice, a further step is also required, namely, *what change is necessary to inform my practice?* Being reflective is therefore something more than just a descriptive account of something, as this merely shows up our competency in that area. The interrogative process of re-examining an event or experience is meant to enhance our understanding of it in order to evaluate our learning and thereby enhance our practice. Reflection is therefore an aid to self-development and improved professional practice. The reflective process should therefore be engaging and proactive as we think about the incident since the process seeks to enhance our understanding and learning.

While we draw on a range of different knowledge sources to inform our work with service users, our professional practice is also mediated through the type of person we are, or what is often termed 'use of self'. The following activity is designed to help you reflect about your own self-awareness and the kind of image you might project as a worker.

ACTIVITY 4.8

Think of a metaphor or a simile (a comparative description) to describe how you see yourself as a social worker. For instance, you might see yourself as the hand that steadies the fall, or that social work is like walking through treacle.

Write this down, and if you can, share this activity with another colleague and explain why you choose this metaphor.

- *What does it tell you about yourself?*
- *Does this description of your role impact on your work with service users and colleagues?*
- *What can you do to foster and maintain or adapt this view of yourself?*

Comment

Being reflective takes time – it is a contemplative exercise, so it may well be that you need time to reflect on the metaphor you chose and consider, in terms of developing your self-awareness, the type of worker you are and what knowledge or skills you need to develop. On the other hand, the metaphor you have chosen may illustrate very clearly the view you have of social work and how much this impacts on your practice.

Linking theory with practice

If reflection represents an interrogative process through asking questions to explore and seek a better understanding of the event or experience, then one of the ways of examining the experience is to make it problematic, or to create a *disjuncture* (Light and Cox, 2001).

Bolton (2005) uses the analogy of *through the looking glass* to describe the process of making problematic our experience by examining it, but then we step through the looking glass to see the experience from a different perspective and begin to see that it can be seen and interpreted differently.

So, it is the 'experience', which can be subject to the reflective process be it:

- our practice

- our interactions with service users or colleagues

- our professional role

- our thoughts

- our feelings

- our memories

- spiritual elements.

They are all open to interrogation and what is familiar can become unfamiliar through the looking glass, and what was certain may become uncertain as we acknowledge different interpretations. But the interpretative process is constructive – reflection has a purpose and that is to enhance our understanding and improve our learning and hence our practice. Creating this disjuncture between what is familiar and taken for granted and subjecting it to query and interrogation enables you to re-examine the experience with greater vision. It can offer you an insight into:

- motives

- thoughts and feelings

- new ways of practice.

The metaphor activity is designed as a reflective exercise to help you think in different ways about your view about social work practice or yourself as a practitioner. It should enable you to make links with social work theory and the issues covered in this book, for instance understanding formal and informal theories about the nature of social work and examining the views that you hold, or thinking about the value base of social work, or how organisational structures can impact on your role. However, 'theory' as we know does not just relate to 'formal' theories about social work, but we can gain an insight and understanding from television programmes or films or from reading novels, as well as drawing on our personal experience and the experience of our peers and colleagues.

Moon (1999) identifies a hierarchy of learning which is useful for enhancing our understanding of the reflective process. The hierarchy consists of;

- noticing

- making sense

- making meaning

- working with meaning

- transformative learning (pp136–46).

Reflection is part of a process of developing our understanding and learning and since good learning involves the process of evaluation, we need to 'revisit' this experience or event. Such experiences may be new or significant or they might be 'common' experiences that we are familiar with, but they require our attention as part of the process of continuous professional development. So 'noticing' refers back to identifying an experience to begin the reflective process. In being able to describe and explain an incident or experience, we are attempting to 'make sense' but it is the third stage of 'making meaning' that begins the reflexive process, where we are able to draw on the range of knowledge sources we use in our practice and take the journey 'through the looking glass' to re-examine our behaviour and what we know and consider alternative meanings and understanding. At this stage, you are 'working with meaning' and begin to reflect on and consider new ways of understanding. Moon (1999, p139) also states that this could be a process of *thinking over things until they make better meaning*. At this stage therefore, we can see why reflection is a contemplative process as well, as we need time to accommodate different ways of meaning, otherwise we risk not being able to make sense and advance our understanding.

The final stage of transformative learning is not, according to Moon (1999), something that all learners can achieve. As the name suggests, learning is characterised by a substantial new understanding and *appears to be the result of persistent work towards understanding, but there also seem to be times when sudden transformation of understanding can occur* (p139). The colloquial expression of 'the penny dropping' seems apt here, but at this level, it is more just 'something clicking'. Our understanding of something is substantially transformed and we gain a better understanding that has a significant impact on our learning and practice.

The idea of the reflective practitioner implies a practitioner who is prepared to take responsibility for their own learning by developing the skills of reflection and using these new understandings to enhance their practice. In fact we can go further and argue that it is this quality that is important to develop in ourselves, since we cannot just rely on our formal learning or practice experience to develop our professional practice. There are a number of techniques which can be drawn upon to facilitate the reflective process, such as the use of reflective journals, critical incident analysis or action learning sets (see Moon, 1999). However, since social work involves working with people there are fruitful opportunities almost everywhere we look which provide an opportunity to reflect upon our behaviour and ourselves as we work towards developing effective and professional practice in social work.

C H A P T E R   S U M M A R Y

Social work is mediated by its organisational context. It helps to structure our role, guide our practice and influences our interventions with service users. Over the last ten years, contemporary human services organisations, particularly in the field of social care and health, have been driven by government initiatives aimed at modernising services, which emphasise efficiency and effectiveness in terms of identified performance indicators or outcomes. Alongside these performance outcomes, social care and health organisations are expected to provide services that are considered 'service user focused', which promote their independence and increase their control over the services they require and which require the establishment of partnership working between the service user, the worker and other professionals or agencies involved in providing services. These changes have shaped the organisational context of social work practice resulting in the establishment of separate social services in child care and adult services that are concerned to promote greater collaborative and inter-professional practices between different agencies providing support. At the same time, management structures have been heavily criticised for an overreliance on aggressive styles of managerialism that emphasise legalistic and procedural concerns which *tend to reinforce mechanistic practice rather than creativity and innovation* (Stepney, 2000, p12). In contrast, management structures that favour a human relations approach provide a greater opportunity to realign social care organisations back towards the values of social care and place the needs of the service user as pivotal to effective practice in organisations. Such organisations are indicative of learning organisations which value their workforce as key to an effective organisation. Managing the workforce is therefore an important part of professional practice and while supervision can be seen as an important and vital structure for facilitating effective practice in line with the organisations goals, the concept of the reflective practitioner stresses the individual qualities that a social worker should aspire to develop so that they can be an active participant in the development of their own professional practice.

FURTHER READING

Coulshed, V and Mullender, A with Jones, D and Thompson, N (2006) *Management in social work*. 3rd edition. Basingstoke: Macmillan.
This provides comprehensive coverage of the issue of management and social work and can act as a valuable resource for both practitioner and manager in developing their skills and knowledge in this area.

Knott, C and Scragg, T (eds) (2007) *Reflective practice in social work*. Exeter: Learning Matters.
This provides a good introduction to understanding the concept of reflective practice and developing your knowledge and skills in order to enhance professional practice in social work.

WEBSITES

www.scie.org.uk
The Social Care Institute for Excellence provides an excellent web-based resource and is concerned to disseminate knowledge-based good practice guidance; and involves service users, carers, practitioners, providers and policy-makers in advancing and promoting good practice in social care.

Chapter 5
Putting theory into practice

3.2.2.3 Analysis and synthesis.
3.2.4 Skills in working with others.
Involve users of social work services in ways that increase their resources, capacity and power to influence factors affecting their lives.

Introduction

In this final chapter, I bring together some of the themes which have developed in this book and consider how they can be utilised in a practice setting. In other words, I am looking at making more explicit the links between theory and practice in social work. So, remembering that theories represent explanatory frameworks for helping us 'make sense' of the situation in question, and help structure our thinking, we can see that theories are central to helping us make sense of our practice and what we do. Theories, as explanatory frameworks, represent coherent ideas and assumptions that guide our thinking and influence our practice. This emphasises the relationship between our thinking and what we do, or put more formally, the relationship between theory and practice.

In Chapter 2, I put forward my view about the nature of social work and suggested that social work should be part of a socially emancipatory project which draws upon an alternative discourse associated with an empowerment approach. Such a view advocates that social work should move beyond merely a focus on the individual and that it should also seek to promote greater social equality and participation, particularly for those members of society who are vulnerable, disadvantaged or marginalised; that is, those who make up the majority of users of social services. By a focus on the disadvantaged and marginalised, social work should contribute towards greater social justice for all society's members.

When I say that social work should be part of this emancipatory ideal, I am of course making a value judgement about the purpose or nature of social work. Different views represent competing explanations about the purpose of social work and at their core, therefore, represent competing beliefs. Therefore questions about values and ethics are always central to any question about the purpose of social work. If we fail to acknowledge their presence, it is only because we find favour with that perspective and therefore take it for granted as unproblematic, or else we are not prepared to engage in a critical process about the purpose of social work. So, from an emancipatory perspective, the purpose of social work should go beyond a *maintenance approach* or the *individualist–reformist* view about social work (Payne, 2005, p9). Instead, social work should align itself with empancipatory approaches that seek to empower the service user (Dominelli, 2002).

In addition, you will also consider the use of an approach to learning known as an issue-based approach (to learning) (IBL). This represents a particular construction about the process of learning that emphasises the active role of the learner in constructing knowledge that is meaningful to them and increases their understanding. It is seen as an 'active' approach to learning that encourages reflexivity in the learner by encouraging you to think about what you have learnt and how this can be used to inform your practice. An IBL therefore supports the link between theory and practice by encouraging us to think about what we have learnt and how this can be used to support our practice.

By the end of this chapter, you should be able to:

- understand what is meant by the term 'empowerment' and the practice implications of adopting this approach;

- recognise the centrality of values and ethics in shaping the construction of social work, and in particular, the use of virtue ethics as a determining guide to practice;

- understand constructions of how we learn, using an issue-based approach to learning (IBL);

- the relationship between theory and practice, using the strengths perspective as an example.

Defining empowerment

We know that a theory represents an explanatory framework which attempts to help us make sense of something – in our case, to help us make sense of and enhance our understanding of questions about the nature of social work. Social theories provide us with competing explanations about the nature of society, and represent explanations on a continuum from an interpretivist view to a structuralist approach. They provide us with an explanation about the relationship between the individual and society and therefore provide us with an understanding of how social problems can occur and that this can represent a disjunction between the individual and their social context. However, it is the process of understanding and critical review that allows us the opportunity to evaluate their competing explanations and we can apply this same process of critical review to concepts such as 'empowerment', which is part of the new or 'emancipatory values' of contemporary social work practice (see Chapter 3).

We know that the term 'empowerment' has also been appropriated by those who are more concerned with curtailing the state's responsibility for welfare in favour of promoting individual responsibility over collective need. Therefore the term has also been used as part of the discourse of individual rights and responsibilities.

CASE STUDY

Margaret is able to use the Direct Payment scheme to construct a care package that suits her self-identified care needs. The Direct Payment scheme originates from the neo-classical economic discourse (Healy, 2005), or what I have termed the individual rights and responsibilities discourse, which favours the promotion of alternative forms of welfare provision and the idea of consumer choice and individual empowerment. Here Margaret becomes the consumer, able to make a choice about her care needs based on a variety of different service provisions and to meet the care needs that she herself has identified. An increase in choice has opened up alternative provisions for Margaret, and not just left her with the limited provision of social services in the form of a day centre. The Direct Payment scheme helps to facilitate Margaret's sense of control or empowerment by removing her reliance on a day centre, as a particular type of service provision which rests on fixed views about older people whereby their care needs are met by an institu-tionalised and universal service.

So, like all concepts, empowerment needs to be considered in a context. In this book, the context that shapes the view that is adopted is that social work is part of an emancipatory ideal based on a belief for greater social equality for society's disadvan-taged members. This moves empowerment beyond an individual focus, which is typical of the individualist–reformist view of social work and the individual rights and responsibilities discourse. Instead the approach adopted in this book is more in keeping with Howe's (1987) description of the role of the social worker as a *raiser of consciousness*. Social workers supporting an empowering approach to their practice seek social change at both an individual and a social level and this represents an alternative discourse where social work is concerned with the promotion of social equality or social justice in favour of those groups and individuals who can be described as vulnerable, disadvantaged or marginalised – that is, those individuals and groups who typically make up the majority of users of social services.

Social work is well placed to adopt this wider emancipatory perspective since it med-iates between the individual and society, and therefore our work should contribute towards a more enhanced society. This is true for all perspectives about the purpose of the social work (given the centrality of values and ethics in considering the purpose of social work). However, in this book, a 'more enhanced society' is one that is concerned with promoting greater social equality and participation in favour of society's most vulnerable and marginalised members. Our mediatory role between the state and society and the individual is also one of social work's key strengths, as this allows us to consider more closely the relationship between the individual and society, and how far our work contributes to a society in which that individual feels more inte-grated. Since social work typically involves people who are socially excluded, this provides the rationale for providing an empowerment perspective within social work. Our mediatory role therefore allows us to consider the repertoire of interperso-nal skills and values that we develop as social workers and also consider how far the work we do enables us to contribute towards a social justice goal.

Virtue ethics as a guide to informing our relationship with service users

Thinking about what the goal or purpose of social work should be demands more than just a consideration of our role *vis-à-vis* the service user and carer, and turns the spotlight on us, as students or practitioners of social work, and demands the adoption of a critically reflective focus. In doing so, we ask ourselves what kind of society we want our work to contribute towards and this requires an informed view concerning theories about the nature of society and how they inform a view about the nature of social work. We have a moral responsibility to think critically about competing views of social work, as the approach of social constructionism highlights the influence of importance factors, such as context, time and legislation, for instance, which can alter our construction and understanding of what we define as the domain of social work and the role of the worker. In addition, the values of anti-discriminatory practice encourage the development of appropriate practice skills and knowledge that acknowledge the impact of structural processes rather than just an individual focus. Social work is not a free-floating or neutral activity but is engulfed in questions about values and ethics and the decisions that professionals make which affect people's lives. Although social work is a socially mandated and purposeful activity, it is carried out by individuals driven, at least in part, by what we believe to be the purpose of social work. We should therefore be clear about what we personally think our role should be as well as being clear about what is expected of us, and what we think we can offer. This calls to mind the centrality of values and ethics in the role of social work, since we are in fact asking what are the values we consider important for professional practice. The approach I am emphasising in this context is the importance of virtue ethics and how we feel we ought to behave (see Chapter 3). An emphasis on virtues or the quality of our character underpins the centrality of the interpersonal relationship in social work.

ACTIVITY **5.1**

Which virtues or values do you think are necessary to develop as part of developing a virtuous character in social work, and what qualities might you identify as part of supporting a social justice view of social work?

Comment

There are a number of values that I think are important to cultivate as part of being a good or virtuous social worker. Firstly, personal qualities such as honesty and keeping people informed of what is going on; reliability, for instance, doing what we say we will do, and managing our time by not missing appointments or turning up late; and personal integrity are important. In virtue ethics, the site of moral integrity rests with the worker and forces us to think critically about our behaviour and to ask ourselves whether we have behaved in ways in which we feel we have done the best we could. Personal or moral integrity is about issues of accountability and responsibility concerning our actions or behaviour. It is therefore important to think carefully about what type of behaviour we feel is important in social work and what might be expected of us. This calls to mind a consideration of the expectations of the organisations that we work in as well as what our service users might expect from us and how we deal with these expectations. In fact expectations about how we ought to behave (that is, questions about ethical behaviour) can often result in competing demands, and Figure 3.1 reminds us of this potential for conflict. This is why virtue ethics are important, as they encourage us to think reflexively about our behaviour and that we should be able to explain and justify our behaviour.

In thinking about a social justice view of social work and the virtues or qualities that might help promote this, the skill of critical enquiry is important and is part of what Brown and Rutter (2006) refer to as habits of mind (see Chapter 1) that support the development of critical thinking and reflection.

In exploring competing views about the nature of society and the resultant different views about the nature and purpose of social work, we have began to explore the relationship between theory and practice in social work, that is, how different explanations about the nature of society can result in different practice outcomes. However, the process of critical review (which is part of the skill of critical enquiry) involves considering how dominant discourses and explanations can reinforce commonly taken-for-granted assumptions about social problems and the difficulties people encounter. Having a commitment towards a social justice view requires an appreciation of alternative discourses that do not reinforce individual culpability, but instead recognise how different life chances result in qualitatively different life experiences and therefore require a diversity of responses informed by an appreciation of different explanations to help make sense of what is going on and how best to support people in need. It is, as I have said, a value judgement about the type of society we want our work to contribute towards. In fact, the complexity of virtue ethics makes them an ideal accompaniment to the characterisation of contemporary social work as dealing with complexity, uncertainty and risk. Virtue ethics place the worker centre stage in a critical process of engaging in questions about the nature of social work and the relationship between the worker, service user and others involved in their care and the provision of services. In thinking critically about these questions, we begin to take more responsibility for our work by thinking about the type of society we want our work to contribute towards, and thus what type of social work agency and the qualities of ourselves and other workers that will most facilitate this. In doing so, we begin to look more critically at the work setting and support networks that can be cultivated and utilised, as well as questions about efficiency and effectiveness, and the management of practice and what types of organisations can best facilitate this (see chapter 4).

Virtue ethics do not displace or undermine a consideration of duty or consequential based ethical approaches. However, they do stand as an important corrective to the tendency in heavily biased managerial settings which can characterise contemporary practice, to minimise or distance ourselves from a consideration of the rightness of our behaviour, since *principle-based approaches* (Banks, 2006) are more concerned with action or outcome, and rely less on a consideration of the integrity of the person undertaking the action.

Linking theory with practice using an issue-based approach to learning

So far, I have explored the importance of thinking critically about views about the nature and purpose of social work and linking this with an empowerment approach about the nature and purpose of social work. In addition, I have argued about the centrality of values and ethics in determining our role and how we behave, and in particular, identified the importance of virtue ethics as highlighting the importance of 'self' in the social work process. In this section we continue to think about the links between theory and practice by emphasising the importance of a learning approach that encourages deep-rooted or meaningful learning as central to the process of helping to 'make sense' of what we are learning so that it can be used constructively to help aid our understanding.

One way of linking theory with practice is through the use of a learning technique known as an issue-based approach to learning (IBL) (Bolzan and Heycox, 1998). An IBL is a variant of problem-based learning (PBL) and is an approach to learning and teaching that aims to promote deep-rooted or meaningful learning, alongside a concern to develop a critically reflective and analytic practitioner. Such an approach encourages us to think about the ideas that inform our practice so that we become aware of the relationship or link between theory and practice and therefore we are in a better position to critique our standpoint and those of others. In developing this awareness, we attempt to make sense and increase our understanding.

As an innovative learning technique, the concept of PBL has a history going back over 100 years and is widely attributed to the work of Dewey (1859–1952), the American philosopher and educator, who was concerned with changing the focus from what people learnt to how they learnt. It is essentially a constructivist approach to learning *based on students' active participation in problem-solving and critical thinking regarding a learning activity that they find relevant and engaging.* In other words, learners construct, or develop their own knowledge by *testing ideas and approaches based on their prior knowledge and experience, applying these to a new situation and integrating the new knowledge joined with pre-existing intellectual constructs* (Briner, 1999, cited in Gibbons and Gray, 2002, pp530–1). This describes a cognitive process whereby new learning is assimilated and accommodated. We are able *to make sense of the new learning and what is known. Accommodation results in meaningful learning and understanding* (Moon, 1999, p143).

Moon (1999, p143) goes on to give several examples of how this process of understanding is typically expressed in everyday language.

- *Ah, now you have told me that, I can understand it!*

- *So, for these reasons, I can see why I must do it in this way.*

- *This ties in with what I have been thinking.*

- *I understand the reasoning behind this sequence now.*

An issue-based approach therefore helps to promote deep or meaningful learning and understanding. It is the term adopted here rather than 'problem-based learning', which can be problematic in social work, particularly if social work is viewed as part of an emancipatory perspective concerned with the promotion of social change and justice. Bolzan and Heycox (1998), suggest that the use of 'problems' is unnecessarily pathologising and suggestive of a solution, when in fact social work is characterised by risk and uncertainty and requires a diversity of responses and therefore, an 'issue-based approach to learning' is adopted here.

We know that our ideas and beliefs impact on our practice, and therefore we might expect to see some demonstration of these views in terms of practice outcomes. Through the use of case studies and reflective activities an issue-based approach to learning has been adopted in order to encourage a reflexive process of thinking about what you are reading and to encourage you to think about how the ideas discussed can be used to help develop a critical appreciation of the link between social work theories and practice and to consider ways in which you can work proactively with service users. The activities are designed to encourage you to consider how what you have learnt can promote empowering strategies that support the needs of service users and carers. This is based on the premise that social work is an applied subject and therefore a central question to consider when reading and undertaking the activities is *how does this newly acquired knowledge enable me to understand and work proactively with my service user?*

Although IBL is based on constructivist beliefs that people construct a knowledge base that is relevant to their practice, learning is a more dynamic and active process since you do not come to the subject of social work without some system of ideas and beliefs. So, as you engage in the reading and activities, you begin the process of making sense that leads to a fuller understanding. Effectively new knowledge construction is the outcome of the process of knowledge deconstruction and reconstruction, as the new learning or knowledge impacts on what was already known and challenges our thinking and assumptions. This deconstructed knowledge is then critically reconstructed, constructing a new knowledge base that is both broader and more reflexive than what was known before. Learning and understanding become a cycle of critical review and engagement that emphasises the relationship between thinking and doing.

In Chapter 2, when considering the influence of informal theories and their contribution towards practice, you were asked to reflect and think critically about your practice and consider the following questions.

- What are the bases of the ideas that inform my practice?

- Are there alternative explanations for understanding what is going on?

- What have I learnt about my practice?

- What strategies can I develop to improve my work?

This reflective exercise provides an example of *knowledge construction*, as cited by Gibbons and Gray (2002), since it encourages you to engage with your prior knowledge and experience and attempt a synthesis, or bringing together, with the new knowledge acquired. The activities and case studies provide opportunities for you to review your learning and consider the topic in relation to the development of practice skills as well. Knowledge and skill acquisition is seen as a process of development where mastery is not just a technical outcome but is a critically intellectual process as well.

We can see this process of development in the case study of Fiona, which also appears in Chapter 2, as she attempts to make sense of her first placement experience and struggles to understand the dismissive attitude of some of her colleagues. With some support from her practice teacher, Fiona is able to critically assess the learning and skills she has developed so far while on placement and also to consider the context in which social work is practised and experienced. In so doing she becomes less quick to judge those workers whose behaviour or attitude is less than exemplary. Fiona's ability to reflect on her experience not only demonstrates the importance of critical reflection and analysis, and the need to consider alternative explanations for behaviour, but also reminds us of the importance of virtue ethics as an underpinning practice philosophy.

McBeath and Webb (2002) suggest some key virtues necessary for effective social work, namely:

- judgement
- experience
- understanding
- reflection
- disposition.

As Fiona's case demonstrates, in developing an understanding, we do not necessarily condone, either in relation to service users or colleagues, but rather, the process of understanding allows us to begin to make sense and provide an explanation that can allow a working relationship to develop so that change is possible. The virtue of disposition also allows us to critically assess a situation, or in Fiona's case, the team she is working in. Fiona was able to form a revised judgement about her colleagues, which perhaps was less critical than her original feelings, and also provided a means of helping Fiona evaluate the type of setting and the values of practice that she would most thrive in, an agency more in keeping with a learning organisation (see Chapter 4).

As part of the process of critically examining the ideas that inform our practice, Fiona is encouraged to deconstruct some of the many ideas and beliefs that go to make up the contested activity that is social work. In turn, she is able to acknowledge the validity of much of her learning from the team in helping her develop her practice experience and in doing so, she becomes less critical of some of the dismissive comments made by some of her colleagues. However, Fiona's own value position of supporting an empowering or proactive approach to practice, means that she retains a critical focus on how far social work practice and theories reinforce or challenge oppressive views about service users and their circumstances. In critically reviewing her experiences and knowledge, Fiona reconstructs her understanding, resulting in a deeper construction or understanding of her view about the purpose of social work. She has sought a way of making sense and understanding behaviour that does not reinforce a stigmatising view of people who use services. In being able to deconstruct the ideas and beliefs that have developed among some of the team, Fiona is able to recognise competing discourses about the nature of social work. She interrogates the knowledge sources in ways which are *sensitive to contextual dimensions and marginalised voices* (Parton, 2002, p243). For Parton (2002), this process of critical review and interrogation recognises *that, while multiple discourses might be available, only a few are heard and are dominant, these being intimately related to the dominant powers/knowledges* (p243). Fiona is able to evaluate her experiences and understanding and now has a more sophisticated understanding of social work. Her experience in her first placement not only reinforces her commitment to an empowering approach but she also recognises the complexity associated with contemporary practice and that workers too can be negatively affected by their working conditions and poor management of their practice, alongside a lack of material resources that can result in uncritical and routine practice. Workers need supportive environments in which to practise creatively. Fiona is sensitive therefore to the 'context' of contemporary practice as witnessed through her first placement experience. However, her commitment to a social justice view about social work means that she prefers an alternative discourse which favours an empowering approach to practice and challenges the focus on individual rights and responsibilities. Instead it looks towards social change based on collective rights and responsibilities and is therefore part of a critical discourse to understanding individual and social problems.

Using Fiona as an example of an issue-based approach to learning, we can see how Fiona learns to appreciate that social work is a contested activity with competing views about its purpose. Even though Fiona 'knew' this 'in theory', the reality of her practice experience forced her to reconsider these competing views and perhaps, most importantly, evaluate their validity. Fiona engaged in a process of knowledge deconstruction and reconstruction as she critically examined and evaluated different and competing knowledge sources, such as practice wisdom and her 'lived' experience of 'doing' social work, informal and formal theories about social work's purpose and how to do social work, alongside a consideration of the values that she believes are important in professional social work. In Fiona's case study, we can see how values and ethics lie at the heart of questions about the nature of social work. Together, these sources of knowledge have impacted on Fiona and helped her construct a knowledge base that is more enhanced and appreciative of the complexity of contemporary social work practice. For Fiona, learning has become a reflexive process of critical review and engagement and one that impacts on her practice.

Sakamoto and Pinter (2005) address some of the limitations of anti-oppressive practice (AOP) and in particular point out *its lack of focus at a micro and individual level* (p435). They argue that AOP should not only be concerned with macro social change in favour of marginalised and disadvantaged groups, but that workers must also address and be aware of the power differentials that exist at an individual level and its impact on the professional relationship. In this respect, they point to the need for the worker to be critical about the nature of the interpersonal relationship between themselves and the service user and the need for the worker to develop *critical consciousness.* They define this as *the process of continuously reflecting upon and examining how our own biases, assumptions and cultural worldviews affect the ways we perceive difference and power dynamics* (p441). How to engage in this process is identified, and the authors view this as an integral element of an AOP framework. Critical consciousness is therefore a means of helping to raise social workers' awareness of power differentials that may affect their role with service users. Power is something that is identified as something that can be used productively with service users to promote positive changes for them, but equally, critical consciousness can be used to support and help social workers who are also members of marginalised and disadvantaged groups to feel more empowered personally and professionally. In their more enlightened state, workers can perform more effectively in their professional role and work towards social action and greater social justice.

A proactive approach to practice

A proactive approach to practice is one based on supporting individuals and groups in gaining greater control over their lives and a greater sense of social participation in local environments. It is a means of increasing a person's sense of effectiveness over their circumstances. A proactive approach therefore describes an empowerment approach to social work practice. Empowerment is thus a process as well as an outcome.

Parker and Randall (1997) describe 'empowerment' as belonging to a family of words, which include:

- partnership
- participation
- enabling
- and facilitating.

They are all concerned with creating a language of change at both a micro and macro level.

There is a sense of multi-level change in the term 'empowerment' that is seen as part of a process that makes it possible for people to exercise power and have more control over their lives and greater participation and involvement in institutions, agencies and situations that affect them (Croft and Beresford, 1993). Adams (2003) also describes empowerment as a process of becoming powerful. However, as part of the process of critically examining the ideas or theories that inform your practice, you are encouraged to be reflective and re-examine those ideas that go to make up the contested activity that is social work. One such idea is of course the term 'empowerment' and this is a term that is used by both those who support an individual rights and responsibilities discourse, as well as those who support an empowerment approach. Therefore we need to critically re-examine this and consider how far it contributes towards an emancipatory ideal. Therefore if empowerment refers to a process of *becoming powerful* (Adams, 2003), if we attempt to deconstruct this term, it is useful to think of its opposite, namely *being powerless*. Consider the following activity.

ACTIVITY 5.2

Write down any adjectives or feelings that describe what being powerless means to you.

Comment

You may have identified a number of feelings, or adjectives for describing what being powerless means to you. Here are a number of words that describe this feeling for me.

- Frightened

- Intimidated

- Unworthy

- Isolated

- Lonely

- Unvalued

- Anxious

- Disregarded and ignored.

All these terms are themselves powerful and emotive reminders about the vulnerabilities that many of our service users may experience. Once we can imagine what being powerless feels like, we are engaging in a process of critical reflection and utilising the skill of empathy by considering how our practice can help minimise feelings of powerlessness. So being punctual, for example, or advocating on behalf of our service users, are not just examples of professional standards that we are expected to adhere to, but they are also the virtues we adopt in trying to promote a more positive sense of wellbeing for our service users and carers because these are the values we believe in ourselves and we would want to be treated in this way as well. We treat our service users with respect and dignity, not because they are 'duties' but because we do not want them to feel unvalued or their feelings disregarded. Such reflective thinking can contribute towards an empowering approach towards service users. So, for instance, treating a person as an individual, rather than as 'a case', listening to their story and respecting their views, providing the person with clear and accurate information, asking them what they want rather than assuming we know best, and providing a choice as to where to meet, all provide examples of developing an empowering approach to social work which is service-user focused and helps facilitate a sense of control over the social work process. In fact these identified qualities are among those that have been consistently identified by service user groups and carers as attributes most desired in care workers in order to promote greater service user independence and participation in the decision-making process (see Croft and Beresford, 2002).

ACTIVITY 5.3

Having identified some feelings which describe a sense of powerlessness for you, now consider some of the ways that these same feelings may be experienced by service users that you work with.

• How might these feelings impact on your professional relationship with them?

Comment

Feelings such as 'frightened' and 'intimidated' capture the sense of 'anxiety' that can be evoked when social workers become involved in service users' lives. This can represent the sense of stigma that often surrounds social work involvement due to social work's association with people who are encountering difficult situations or where their behaviour is the source of concern that has prompted our involvement. This can result in a feeling of 'failure' for the service user because they may feel that their coping strategies have been ineffective and contribute to a sense of 'unworthiness' and that their capabilities are not valued. Equally, feeling frightened or intimidated may capture the sense of anxiety surrounding social work involvement because service users may not understand the social work process and are anxious about the implications or consequences of social work involvement.

Following this, the circumstances surrounding social work involvement can often result in service users and carers feeling a 'lack of control' over the social work process leading to feelings that their contributions may be 'disregarded' or 'ignored', compounding feelings of 'isolation' and a sense that the situation is moving beyond their control. This can result in the development of care plans that service users feel do not adequately meet their needs and ultimately may lead to service users withdrawing from the social work process. This can have two unfortunate consequences: either social work involvement may feel 'intrusive' for the service user, due to the concerns about their situation, or social work involvement may be withdrawn, due to the perceived lack of commitment by the service user. Both these outcomes may result in reinforcing a social worker's view about individual culpability and 'blaming the victim' or, for the service user, may contribute towards a sense of social work being either 'over-controlling' or ineffective. For the social worker and the user of the service, their perception of each other does little to raise the standard of professional practice or contribute towards empowering practice in social work.

We can see therefore that a key element of empowerment is that it is a process – something to engage with – but also that the notion of empowerment is based on assumptions of strength. Looking back to the suggestion that empowerment is about people taking control (Croft and Beresford, 1993), if they have not experienced much control over their lives, then they may also need support. In our role as a social worker, we should therefore facilitate this process. If we go back to the idea that empowerment is part of a language of change, then how do we facilitate change in our service user?

Utilising the skills of reflection and empathy, we can imagine for ourselves the process of facilitating change, by asking the following questions.

- What makes you take action in the first place?

- What gives you the courage to believe in your ability to carry out your plan?

- How do you translate the personal into the political – that is, an idea into a reality?

If you believe the task is impossible, then it is unlikely that you will take any action at all. Equally, if you feel your abilities are insignificant and not valued, then it is less likely that you will feel able or motivated to make a change. In these cases, you may well feel deflated and give up, feeling defeated and, possibly, powerless. However, if empowerment is a process of becoming powerful, then we need to believe that our actions can make a difference and that we are capable of taking action and using resources to benefit ourselves. We are therefore likely to experience a feeling of empowerment if we feel we are effective and competent and have a sense of power and control over our lives. Empowerment is thus premised on a sense of positive self-esteem. We therefore need a perspective of hopefulness and an ability to use resources effectively in order to promote a sense of capability that is suggestive in the term 'empowerment'.

So far, I have suggested a process of personal reflection and empathy in order to call to mind what is required in moving towards an empowerment approach in our practice, but what of the service user? Empowerment certainly seems a valid principle to imbue our service users with, but given that the majority of service users can be characterised by their vulnerability, social disadvantage and marginalised status, they may well feel more disempowered than powerful. Since empowerment is a process, it therefore takes time, energy and commitment. It is possible that acting alone as a social worker, you will be unable to facilitate such a change without tapping into a wider pool of community resources that enable the service user to flourish and develop their self-confidence and social competence. Part of those resources will be the organisations in which social workers work. A proactive or empowering approach to practice is therefore premised on the belief in service user participation in order to change and improve social care services.

This involves a commitment to developing collaborative alliances with service user forums and promoting more inclusive workplaces and practices. Service user perspectives have a long history in challenging the traditional view of social work as 'expert' and have sought to increase service user involvement and participation in the design and delivery of services so that they are representative of users' needs and non-stigmatising (see Croft and Beresford, 2002).

RESEARCH SUMMARY

Recent research by the Social Care Institute for Excellence (SCIE) highlights nine areas that service users identify as helping to make a difference and how practice can be improved. A summary of the findings is presented below.

- *Users need feedback on their participation. A lack of feedback can have a negative effect on how people feel about being involved and the difference this can make.*

- *Changes can start with just one person. It can be difficult to feel part of a change strategy if you do not feel as though you are going to be affected by that change. Individual service users or service users' groups may feel unsupported and find it difficult to speak up about their concerns. Although formal complaint procedures may exist, people may still remain unaware of them or find them difficult and intimidating to use.*

- *Involving users in different ways. Service users want to be involved not only in terms of shaping service plans and policies but they also want to be involved in developing services in partnership with organisations as well.*

- *Making sure everyone gets the chance to be involved. Service user involvement needs to be representative of all user groups and to acknowledge differences in terms of issues such as culture or sexuality, for instance.*

- *Power relations. Differences in power and influence between social care professionals and service users can make it difficult for service users to be listened to seriously.*

- *What the organisation wants and what the service user wants. Sometimes there are competing demands between these two views, or there may be resource implications which make it not possible to make the changes advocated by service users. Organisations need to make it clear what can and what cannot be done.*

- *Getting people to participate takes time and resources. Both sides need to discuss timetables and ways of working which provide everyone with opportunities to join in. Workers need support to enable them to think about service users' concerns and their participation.*

- *Organisational commitment. If organisations are serious about service user participation they need to make their organisations more responsive to service user involvement.*

- *Benefits of participation. While service users may gain something from participation and involvement, it is also important to consider what the change strategy has achieved.*

(Taken from Position Paper 3: Has Service User participation made a difference to social care services? Summary. March 2004, SCIE)

The research indicates the need to develop working environments and professional relationships with service users and carers which support and facilitate their involvement and participation in the construction of services which are meaningful for them. Such a view is compatible with the values of social work and supports an empowerment focus in our practice. Social work outcomes are mainly premised on a belief that human and social power can be used to promote personal, interpersonal and social competence. If empowerment is premised on positive self-esteem, then key to this approach is a focus on service users' strengths and competence. We should be aware that the helping process does not facilitate change when we describe problems in terms of deficits, incompetencies or problems. We need to take into account and acknowledge the reality of the problem, but the problem is not the defining characteristic of the service user, and a predominance on its focus becomes counterproductive to change.

Working from a strengths perspective

The strengths perspective (Saleebey, 2006) supports an empowering approach to social work practice since it seeks to focus on the service user's strengths or potential, rather than a preoccupation with their difficulties or problems. The strengths perspective therefore acts as a powerful counterforce to the tendency in social work to pathologise service users by seeing them as either 'victims' of their disadvantage or makers of their own misfortune, and seeing the social worker as 'expert'. The strengths perspective therefore challenges traditional models of anti-discriminatory or anti-oppressive practice theories that identify aspects of structural inequality as the defining feature of the service user, and seeing them as 'victims' of their disadvantage. Critiques of this view argue that this results in a one-dimensional view of the service user, reducing their identities to essentialist categories, such as 'disabled', 'elderly' or 'black' service users, and can result in the promotion of universal services to meet their needs. Such criticisms have been constructed around a rejection of professionalism and the view of the social worker as 'knowledge expert', and instead, critics have called for oppressed user groups to be involved in the design and delivery of services to meet their self-identified needs and for service users' voices to be used in the construction of theory and practice (Beresford, 2000; Wilson and Beresford, 2000). Equally, the strengths perspective challenges the individual focus of the maintenance approach to social work and the representation of the social worker as 'expert' in the assessment and intervention process. The strengths perspective therefore attempts to work in partnership with service users and carers, supporting them in identifying their protective factors, or sources of resilience, and seeks to develop these as empowering strategies that can promote positive outcomes for the service user.

> *A strengths perspective demands a different way of seeing clients, their environments and their current situation. Rather than focusing exclusively or dominantly on problems, your eye turns toward possibility ... Mobilise clients' strengths (talents, knowledge, capacities, resources) in the service of achieving their goals and visions and the client will have a better quality of life on their terms.*

> (Saleebey, 2006, p1)

(For a fuller evaluation of the strengths perspective and its theoretical basis, see Oko, 2006.) The strengths perspective emphasises a collaborative process between worker and service user. Such an approach is in line with and supports a service user perspective and the research highlighted what users of services value as part of the social work relationship. Adopting this approach we can see that life chances and experiences interact in a unique way, shaping the development of self. The focus on life experiences emphasises the interpersonal dynamic of social work. When we are looking at strengths we are concerned with how experiences have shaped us and how we have dealt with them, as this can provide inspiration and meaning and the basis of collaborative work. We move towards looking at people's coping and adaptive skills and levels of resilience, whether these are personal qualities, or sources of support from families or communities. The difficulties or the problems that prompt social services' involvement are acknowledged, but they are not the hallmark of people's identity.

Working collaboratively with service users and carers means that they become an integral part of the assessment and intervention process, helping to identify a change outcome which is meaningful for them. Thus the service user and carer are involved in:

• defining their situation;

• determining goals;

• selecting a course of action;

• evaluating results.

As an alternative to a deficit perspective, the lexicon of the strengths perspective talks of possibilities, resilience, resources, transformation and hope. It is premised on the belief in collaboration, partnership and empowerment and requires skills in *dialogue and collaboration and the suspension of disbelief* (Saleebey, 2006, pp14–15) of social workers' persistent negation of clients' views in favour of 'the expert' view, which has been acquired through professional education and training and reliance on traditional formal and informal theories of the client world. Instead, the strengths perspective looks towards valuing the service user's perspective.

In aiming to promote social change in favour of a socially emancipatory perspective, the structural nature of life chances emphasises social work's commitment to collective strategies for social change and thus moves social work beyond an individual focus. A conflict-based analysis of our society reveals the structural nature of many of our service users' difficulties and therefore the importance of collective strategies that shift the emphasis of intervention away from just an individual focus. Such an approach calls to mind the importance and effectiveness of self-help and support groups that unite common experiences with a focus on gaining support and increasing confidence in a non-threatening environment. As experiences are shared, so people learn to appreciate their contributions, skills and talents and perhaps most importantly, that their private difficulties are also commonly experienced. Such an appreciation can combine to promote confidence and social competence in line with an empowerment perspective. As Gutierrez (1994) suggests (cited in DuBois and Miley, 1999), empowerment is about the process of increasing personal, interpersonal or political power so that individuals, families and communities feel able to take action to improve their situation.

Preparing to work from a strengths perspective

ACTIVITY **5.4**

In preparation for adopting a strengths perspective in your work, consider the following questions.
* *What aspects of structural inequality impact on the service user group that you work with?*
* *What knowledge do you need to work with this service user group?*

Comment

Critical sociological theory has identified how aspects of structural inequality impact on service users' lives. So, for instance, the impact of ageism has revealed the persistent marginalisation of issues relating to age, particularly 'old' age, and that *age is not simply a matter of biological maturation – it is a highly significant social indicator*, on the basis of which, *power, privilege and opportunity tend to be allocated* (Thompson, 2006, p98). So, according to our age, we are either ascribed or denied power, privilege and opportunity. Using this example, we need to understand the impact of ageism and the dominance of a medical discourse in shaping welfare provision when we are working with older service users.

Formal knowledge about structural inequality can also be drawn from the insights and experiences of service user perspectives, such as the Disabled People's Movement (DPM), which has been instrumental in politicising the needs of people with disabilities, pointing to social structures which continue to 'dis-able' people with impairments. Instead the DPM advocates the 'social model of disability' as a means of counteracting the traditional individualised view of disability with its focus on the disability as the problem. Knowledge of structural inequalities, such as gender, socio-economic differences, 'race' and ethnicity and disability, and service user perspectives on the impact of their experiences of these inequalities, should go somewhere towards counteracting discriminatory practice with service users and these alternative discourses should not reinforce individual culpability but instead reinforce a commitment to collective strategies in favour of greater social equality.

In addition, we draw on our developing practice experience of working with a particular service user group and this emphasises the importance of reflective thinking and reviewing and evaluating our understanding of contact and involvement with service users. We would also draw upon formal knowledge about relevant welfare legislation and critical use of policies and procedures and how far these are useful in working with service users, as well as knowledge acquired from university study, such as theories of human growth and development and methods of interventions for working directly with service users.

These questions are an important part of preparation for any type of work with service users, perhaps especially so when adopting a strengths perspective in order to counteract a persistent criticism of this approach, namely that it can be interpreted as a naïve approach to practice (Healy, 2005).

Good practice in social work requires us to have knowledge and skills that are useful in the helping process, therefore it is right that we regularly appraise our knowledge and what we bring to our involvement with service users. An understanding of structural inequalities gives us knowledge and an insight into how service users may identify themselves or, indeed, how identities can be foisted upon us. In addition, knowledge and understanding of material disadvantage and structural inequality can go some-way towards acknowledging the social control aspect of statutory social work and that many service users may feel a sense of distrust towards social work involvement, coupled with a fear that we do not understand the complexities of their social lives. Our knowledge of material disadvantage can help to demonstrate that we are pre-pared to acknowledge alternative views that do not reinforce individual culpability or individualise service users' difficulties. The knowledge that we bring to practice situa-tions also has to be translated into a working relationship with service users and this calls to mind a focus on the skills that we can utilise as part of developing a strengths perspective.

ACTIVITY 5.5

Identify some of the practice skills that can be used as part of adopting a strengths perspective with service users.

Comment

Many of the skills that we bring are part of the repertoire of professional practice development in social work. Trevithick (2005) identifies skills that can range from basic to advanced and which can be either generalist or specialist in nature. Out of her list of 50 skills, there are a number worth identifying, such as:

- planning and preparing for interview;
- creating a rapport and establishing a relationship;
- empathy and sympathy;
- offering encouragement and validation;
- empowering and enabling skills;
- working in partnership;
- negotiating and advocacy skills (pp82–3).

We can add to this the generalist skills of communication, such as 'active' listening and hearing; assessment, review and endings; avoiding the use of professional jargon; explaining our professional role and the way in which we wish to work with service users; and being reliable and consistent. Such skills and using our knowledge in competent ways can combine to create a working relationship with service users that helps to demonstrate our trustworthiness and that we behave in ways in which the service user may also identify as trustworthy. Thus service users are clear about our role and involvement in their lives and that we have shown ourselves to be accessible and willing to work with them 'in partnership'.

We can see that the strengths perspective requires practice knowledge and relevant skills, just like any other practice approach. However, like all practice approaches, it stems from a particular view about the purpose of social work, namely, that social work is about client enablement at an individual and community level *to promote equity and justice at all levels of society* (Cowger et al., 2006, p97). At a practice level, this translates into skills necessary for *dialogue and collaboration* and a belief in *the lexicon of strengths* (Saleebey, 2006, pp10–16). It is a belief that individuals and communities *possess assets, resources, wisdom and knowledge that, at the outset, you probably know nothing about . . . To detect strengths, however, you* must *be genuinely interested in, and respectful of, clients' stories, narrative and accounts (p16)*.

In adopting a strengths perspective in your practice, a useful way of 'hearing' the service user's story is by the use of the 'life snake', or *road map* (Parker and Bradley, 2007). It allows the service user 'to tell their story' by highlighting significant events that have impacted on their lives and shaped their identity (see Oko and Jackson, 2007). It is part assessment tool but equally useful in building up a professional relationship. It demonstrates our interest in their lives and illustrates service users' understanding of events that have shaped their lives – it helps them tell their story. The life snake can reveal difficult or traumatic events, but it can also be a powerful visual reminder that 'life goes on' and hence an important part of helping service users to identify their strengths, that is to ask them what resources (including family, friends, community and neighbourhood), skills and abilities they draw upon to help them at times of difficulty, or equally, illuminate the talents or adaptive abilities they have in helping to manage their lives.

So, in utilising a strengths perspective with service users, an important question to ask them is:

- what strengths (talents; interests; qualities; resources; abilities) do you bring that can be drawn upon to help in achieving your goal?

Such a question imparts a sense of belief, on the part of the worker, that the person they are working with has the capacity or potential to manage their lives more effectively. It imbues a sense of possibility that people can have control, or a sense of agency over their lives and that we believe in their ability to do so. It views service users as causal agents in finding solutions to their problems (Payne, 1997, p277). As part of an empowering approach, it is part of a process of *equipping people with personal resources to take power, by developing their confidence, self-esteem, assertiveness, expectations and knowledge and skills* (Croft and Beresford, 1994, cited in Payne, 2005, p301).

ACTIVITY **5.6**

The following case study of Maria illustrates the use of a strengths perspective in practice. In reading it, identify some of the skills and knowledge that Maria drew upon in her work with the service user.

CASE STUDY

Maria worked in a Women's Aid agency that housed women and their children seeking refuge from violent and abusive relationships. One of the women she worked with had arrived for a fourth time at the refuge, along with her two children, aged seven and nine years. She was awaiting rehousing by the local housing department but felt she wanted to return to her partner.

Maria worked from an empowerment perspective (Dominelli, 2002) which acknowledged a conflict analysis about the nature of society and how structural inequalities impact on service users' lives. In particular, Maria acknowledged a feminist perspective as a means of understanding, explaining and undertaking social work practice, informed by feminist theories (Orme, 2002, p218) in order to help her make sense and understand the experiences of women and in particular, to contribute towards her understanding of the issues involved in supporting women involved in violent and abusive relationships. Maria therefore had a commitment to understanding, or theorising as well as a commitment to link her understanding to productive ways of working and engaging with women service users – that is, linking theory with practice. In particular, Maria adopted the use of a strengths perspective since she felt this approach was in line with the organisation's philosophy about promoting women service users' empowerment and challenging the disadvantages that arise from domestic violence and keeping survivors' voices at the heart of the organisation (www.womensaid.org). In this respect, Maria was fortunate to be working in an organisation that shared her beliefs about an empowering perspective in human services. In adopting a strengths perspective, Maria worked closely with the woman, undertaking a counselling role, and together they began to identify the woman's strengths as a means of promoting a more positive view of herself and increasing her self-confidence and self-esteem.

The woman confided in Maria, and told her some of her life story, identifying her skills in organisation and parenting, where she identified her capacity as a mother in bringing up her children, who remained affectionate, confident and sociable and were doing well at school. In addition, the woman also identified her role at work as a supervisor, which demanded leadership and skills of negotiation, delegation and support. In reviewing her work role and parenting skills, the woman was surprised to realise that in fact these skills and qualities had been identified by others, were equally qualities that she herself admired but had overlooked in herself due to the circumstances of her relationship with her violent partner. The woman acknowledged a group of friends she had at work, that she felt able to draw upon as a supportive network and alongside the other skills and qualities she had identified, felt these could be utilised to help her gain a sense of control over her life and begin to plan for moving into her new home without her partner. In addition, Maria was able to help the woman 'reframe' her view of herself as a 'failure' *for returning to the refuge. Instead, Maria concentrated on confirming her courage to leave her violent relationship and her attempt to gain a sense of control over her life. Rather than viewing the return to the refuge as a sign of weakness, the woman began to acknowledge the refuge as a place of safety and comfort, a supportive environment or enabling niche (Saleebey, 2006) where she could return and not experience a sense of humiliation by being termed 'a failure'. Here, the woman had found an enabling niche that did not condone or reinforce her sense of failure, but instead looked towards facil-itating a sense of ability and competence. In addition, the agency also ran an awareness-training programme, aimed at defining domestic violence and identifying and explaining perpetrators' behaviour, so that women could understand behaviour patterns and how they are affected and controlled by men. This was a ten-week programme and the woman attended alongside other women who had experienced violent and abusive relationships. With both individual and collective support, the woman came to recognise and acknowledge her own capacities and strengths and gained support from some of the other women on the course, by sharing experiences and forming new understandings about domestic violence as well as the group providing opportunities for friendship. Over time, the woman began to feel that she was entitled and capable of making choices and to identify the type of lifestyle and relationship that she felt she wanted and that she no longer felt emotionally dependent on her partner.*

Comment

The following are some of the skills and knowledge that can be identified.

- Maria's use of formal knowledge about the nature of society (a conflict analysis) and a theoretical perspective (feminism), which was relevant in her work with the woman who had experienced domestic violence.

- The use of reflective skills by Maria enabled her to make links with her theoretical knowledge and practice preferences. She was prepared to critically think about ideas that enabled her to make sense and have an understanding of the woman's situation and guide her practice.

- The practice skill of counselling draws upon the establishment of a professional relationship between Maria and the woman and a sense of trust between each other to facilitate a productive rapport. Maria will also draw upon the skills identified in the comment following Activity 5.5.

- In using communication and assessment skills, Maria adopts a 'life-story' approach with the woman, listening to her story and inviting her to identify the strengths that she has overlooked in herself.

- The woman is able to identify personal skills and qualities, as well as recognise her role as a mother and supervisor and the skills that she draws upon. She is also able to identify the quality of friendship and that this is an important resource for her.

- The concept of partnership and collaboration in the assessment process means that the service user has identified her goal as a life without her violent partner and the importance of a new home. She begins to see herself as a causal agent and able to exercise control over her life choices.

- Equally, the woman is able to acknowledge the community resource of the refuge as an enabling niche and a means of collective support and social change for women.

- The realisation that 'over time' the woman felt she was able to make choices and exercise a sense of control over her circumstances, demonstrates perhaps a salutary reminder that empowerment is not only an outcome, premised on a value position about the nature and purpose of social work, but also a process which invariably takes time and requires a commitment on the part of the worker.

Integrating theory with practice – an unending process of critical debate and reflection

Maria's case study demonstrates how her view about the nature of society informs her view about the purpose of social work and the range of individual and collective strategies that can be developed in order to enable her service user to feel more empowered and in control of her life opportunities. Maria is also fortunate that her agency supports and promotes an empowerment perspective about the purpose of welfare services and the centrality of the service user perspective in the development of services. We are reminded of the importance of organisations in shaping practice outcomes, and in particular, the importance of leadership and the management of practice and the value base of human services organisations. We can see in Maria's work a commitment to linking theory with practice and the importance of thinking about the type of society we want our work to contribute towards and this is part of the process of being a critically reflective practitioner.

Becoming a critically reflective practitioner is a skill based on utilising a critical knowledge base that needs to be fostered and developed. It is right that we critically appraise our knowledge and practice skills in terms of providing a service that does not reinforce the negative evaluations that typically plague many service users. Thus the cognitive skills required for critical reflection and analysis help contribute towards being a robust worker, since we know social work is not for the faint-hearted.

Social work typically deals with the most disadvantaged and marginalised people in our society: young children involved in fostering and adoption; vulnerable children and adolescents and their families; people on the periphery or involved with offending; people involved in substance misuse; frail and vulnerable older people and their carers; people with chronic mental health problems and those with learning disabilities. They are either people requiring services and support and at risk of abuse or vulnerable to harm and exploitation, or people who are deeply antagonistic and scathing of social work involvement and view their interventions as harmful in their own right and an invasion of their rights and privacy. Dealing with people's lives which have been blighted by emotional or physical abuse or steeped in years of social and economic deprivation lends social work its characterisation of being concerned with risk, complexity and uncertainty. Therefore doing social work requires a level of professional and personal resilience that equips you to deal with its complexities, challenges and strains. It demands thinking about the type of worker you want to be, what the characteristics are that you think are important for social work practice and what contribution your work can make towards the well-being of society. It requires a critical consideration of the type of organisation you want to work in and the support networks, or supportive niches that can be developed, whether these are formal networks, such as supervision, or more informal support, such as your colleagues. Together, these resources can facilitate your personal and professional development. Such a critical process is demanding and engaging, but it lays the groundwork to be able to succeed in a profession that is renowned for its complexities and demands. However, if we are committed to an emancipatory goal, then as workers we need to have skills and knowledge that move beyond a focus on technical competency, and instead support creative responses that engage with the service user and move towards greater social justice.

C H A P T E R   S U M M A R Y

In this chapter, you have explored the development of an emancipatory approach to social work. This draws upon a view of social work that it should move beyond merely a focus on the individual, and should also seek to promote greater social equality and participation for people who are marginalised, disadvantaged and vulnerable, that is, the majority of people who make up users of social services. By a focus on the disadvantaged and marginalised, social work should contribute towards greater social justice for all society's members. This view of social work is often regarded as a radical view which advocates social change or transformation and can be interpreted as a lofty ideal which many practitioners may find difficult to participate in, despite their commitment to such a view. However, I have presented this view of social work as one that still demands the development of practice skills at an individual level and individual change can still result in a ripple effect that can move beyond just a concern with individual needs and part of a collective strategy and therefore part of an empowerment approach to social work. The strengths perspective in social work is presented as an example of practice that seeks to build upon service users' strengths, and therefore is an acknowledgement of their life experience. By working collaboratively, workers also seek the development of *enabling niches* (Saleebey, 2006) where service users can recognise commonalities of experience and lay the groundwork for community-based collective social change. However, like all approaches to social work, the empowerment approach remains part of a value judgement about the nature of social work and therefore we need to be clear about the views and beliefs we hold and how they impact on our practice. The process of critical analysis and reflection therefore remain central to thinking about the link between theory and practice in social work.

FURTHER READING

Payne, M (2005) *Modern social work theory*. 3rd edition. Basingstoke: Palgrave Macmillan.
This is not always an easy text to read but it provides comprehensive coverage to thinking about social work theory and its construction, as well as the range of practice theories that impact on and influence practice in social work.

Saleebey, D (ed.) (2006) *The strengths perspective in social work*. 4th edition. Boston, MA: Allyn & Bacon.
This provides a comprehensive introduction to understanding the strengths perspective. The

collection of chapters provides examples of working from this perspective with different client groups, including working in organisations, work with individuals and communities.

www.criticalthinking.org This is an American website dedicated to the promotion of critical thinking in order to promote essential change in education and society through the cultivation of fair-minded critical thinking. It is a useful resource that provides links to articles and research on critical thinking and ethical reasoning and a wide range of learning resources to support learning.

Conclusion

In this book I have identified some of the formal and informal frameworks of understanding that we use and draw upon to help us begin to make sense of what social work is, in order to support and help us work with service users and carers. You have seen how social work can be understood as a 'contested activity' that draws on different constructions, or understandings about its role and purpose. I have suggested that a useful way for beginning to understand the different views about the nature and purpose of social work is to view social work as performing a mediatory role on behalf of society; that is, social work straddles the space between society and the individual or community, and therefore we need to understand different explanations about the nature of society and the role of the state in welfare. Therefore different theories about the nature of society will give rise to different theories, or conceptualisations about the purpose of social work. In doing so, three main views about the nature and purpose of social work are revealed and the use of the term 'social constructionism' is adopted as a means of understanding the 'fluidity' of different understandings and how important the context is in shaping our understanding of social work as a contested activity. However, the approach of social constructionism is not intended to confuse your understanding of social work as a contested activity, but instead provides an opportunity to see how these different knowledge sources and their explanations can be used dynamically to increase our understanding and hence our ability to work effectively with service users and carers. Explanatory frameworks, or theories, are therefore essential in helping us make sense and offer an explanation of 'what the matter is' and 'what can be done' as we work collaboratively with people who use services.

In supporting the development of your understanding of how theories can be used to inform your practice, I have adopted the use of an issue-based approach to learning which aims to support 'deep' or meaningful learning. This view of learning sees social work as an applied activity and therefore, what we learn should enable us to make better sense of what we do, i.e. our practice. It is a dynamic view about the relationship between learning and understanding and mirrors the approach adopted in this book, that there is a relationship between theory and practice and that we should use our understanding of what we know to improve our practice. It is therefore a proactive approach to learning that uses case studies and reflective activities to develop and support your understanding and to demonstrate that knowledge is a creative and evolving cycle of deconstruction and reconstruction which seeks to build and enhance your understanding. This view of learning, as a means of enhancing our understanding, involves the process of critical analysis and reflection but I have set the context for evaluating our knowledge sources as one based on the view of social work as being concerned to promote both individual change and social change. This acknowledges the view that social work is a contested activity that involves different and competing views about its nature and purpose, but in the end, I have made a value judgement about the purpose of social work, and viewed it as evolving from a conflict analysis of society that draws upon principles of empowerment and virtue ethics to guide its practice. Such a view maintains a critical eye on the integrity of the worker and the importance of the perspective of the service user and their participation and involvement in the construction of services that is needs-led. Such an approach acknowledges the reality of material disadvantages that impact on the lives of many service users and carers, but at the same time, it also recognises the importance of the interpersonal relationship between worker and service user in helping to shape lives in the direction of positive outcomes for users of social services. This is of course one view about the nature and purpose of social work and social constructionism alerts us to be aware of competing views about the purpose of social work. Knowledge is therefore socially constructed; it does not remain fixed or static and we may find our views about social work are also subject to change and reconstruction. This may seem at once both alarming and a challenge but I hope the material in this book will have prompted you to consider that there are alternative perspectives and explanations that shape competing views about social work's role and purpose and that you now have a fuller understanding of the relationship between theory and practice. By taking an active responsibility to critically review and evaluate your knowledge and skills I hope you feel able to find ways of working constructively and conscientiously in developing your professional role as a social worker.

Glossary

Agency A belief that people (in particular, service users) have the capacity or potential to manage their lives more effectively, increasing their sense of control, or of agency over their lives, and that social workers believe in their ability to do so. It views service users as causal agents in finding solutions to their problems – in other words, that people can actively do something to help themselves. As part of an empowering approach, it is part of a process of equipping people with personal resources to take power, by developing their confidence, self-esteem, assertiveness, expectations and knowledge and skills. People are viewed as having the capacity to act in self-determining ways.

Causal agents (*see* **agency**)

Conflict theory One of three approaches to understanding the nature of society (see **consensus theory** and **interpretivist** approach). It is based on a **structuralist approach** which sees society as largely shaping social life. It represents a competing explanation based on the idea that society is structured along lines of inequality, such as income and health, which result in different life chances that result in qualitatively different life experiences. The idea of a shared belief system is doubtful since social differences minimise opportunities for a shared common identity and instead create opportunities for social conflict between and within social groups. Social conflict is therefore seen as inevitable and a legitimate response to social inequality. Conflict theory supports an **emancipatory** view about the purpose of social work.

Consensus theory One of three approaches to understanding the nature of society (see **conflict theory** and **interpretivist approach**). It represents a **structuralist approach** which sees society as largely shaping social life. This approach emphasises the importance of a shared common belief system and the importance of socialisation, initiated first within our family and reinforced through education and the mass media. These beliefs represent dominant norms and values with expectations of conformity. It is this 'consensus' about how we ought to behave that gives society its seeming stability. Social problems are therefore likely to be viewed as the result of individual deviancy or pathology and a deviation from the dominant *status quo*. The consensus approach favours a **maintenance approach** about the nature and purpose of social work.

Critical thinking Being aware of taken-for-granted ideas and encompassing beliefs that frame our understanding of social work and their influence on our practice. Critical thinking involves an awareness of assumptions and their impact, recognising the influence of context, and that there are alternative explanations. Reaching an understanding is based on analysis and reflection of the ideas and beliefs that are under review.

Deep-rooted or meaningful learning Promoting learning that builds upon what has been previously learnt so that the learner is able to 'make sense' of the new learning and gains a fuller understanding of the subject. It is a move away from 'surface' learning where, at best, new learning can only be memorised and carries little sense for the learner.

Deontological One of three ethical theories which underpin beliefs about how social workers ought to behave. This approach emphasises the importance of duty or rights in the decision-making process, and is based on principled beliefs or obligations that are adhered to regardless of consequences. This approach stresses the importance of absolute or fixed principles to guide behaviour which are applied consistently and universally (*see* **utilitarianism–consequentialism** and **virtue ethics**).

Discourse A concept central to the approach of **social constructionism**. It refers to a body of ideas and beliefs that become established as knowledge or an accepted world view. Discourses are drawn upon to help us make sense of our social world and, in turn, they frame or influence our understanding of what we consider to be valid or appropriate ways of thinking and behaving.

Emancipatory approach One of three conceptualisations about the role or purpose of social work (Dominelli, 2002) which supports a **conflict** view about the nature of society. It describes a view about the purpose of social work that is concerned to promote social change and promote greater social equality, particularly for those groups that can be described as vulnerable, marginalised or disadvantaged, that is, the majority of people who make use of social services. It aims to promote greater social equality through individual and collective strategies. Payne (2005) describes this approach as a socialist–collectivist view (*see* **therapeutic–helping approach** and **maintenance approach**).

Empowerment Seen as both a process and an outcome. As a process, it is part of practice methodology that aims to support service users to acquire a sense of power and control over their circumstances, increasing their sense of effectiveness. It belongs to a family of words, which include 'partnership', 'participation', 'enabling' and 'facilitating'. In terms of its outcome, empowerment is concerned with creating a language of change at both a micro (individual) and macro (social) level and is part of an **emancipatory** view about the nature and purpose of social work.

Ethical theory (*see* **deontological, utilitarianism–consequentialism** and **virtue ethics**).

Ethics In contrast to **values**, ethics are more prescriptive and deal with 'what is right and correct' (Loewenberg and Dolgoff, 1992) and represent guidelines or principles about the way we ought to behave. Ethics are the 'putting into action' of the values we believe in.

Formal theory What is typically thought of as 'theory' by students and practitioners. Formal theories are what is written down in texts and represent the ideas that are used to explain and help us understand questions about social work, whether, for example, the text attempts to help make sense of social work education, practice teaching or social work methods of intervention. Such theories represent the ideas that are used to help us make sense, provide explanations and challenge our thinking about social work (*see* **informal theory**).

Human relations management An approach to understanding the structure of an organisation that emphasises the importance of the relationship between people carrying out tasks within the agency as crucial to its success. It emphasises the 'human' aspect of an organisation and that the quality and commitment of the staff are just as important as the management structures to a successful organisation (*see* **managerialism**).

Human services organisations Organisations that employ personnel whose common theme is dealing with people experiencing personal and social problems. Such organisations are mandated by society to serve the interest of the service user as well as those of society.

Individual rights and responsibilities discourse Represents a powerful body of ideas and beliefs that favours a residual or minimum role for the state in welfare. This approach advocates individual responsibility over collective (state) responsibility. An extended role for the state in welfare is seen as fundamentally threatening to the economic and social well-being of a free market economy (i.e. capitalism). This discourse is part of a worldwide movement away from collective action towards the individual marketisation of all aspects of social life. The focus is on the individual in society and emphasises personal responsibility and culpability.

Individualist–reformist view (*see* **maintenance approach**).

Informal theory Informal theories are more difficult to pin down and typically represent taken-for-granted or common-sense ideas and beliefs that are culturally and professionally reinforced through the familial process of socialisation and social relationships; culturally through the mass media, for instance, in newspapers, books, plays, and from watching the television; and from our practice experience. While we get formal explanations for people's behaviour, such as sociological or psychological theories, these ideas also get translated into taken-for-granted and informal or 'common-sense' ideas, such as explanations about so called 'anti-social' behaviour which can be spoken about in terms of individuals 'not being brought up properly'. While informal ideas are not necessarily at odds with formal explanation, there is a danger that they can be based on unquestioned or taken-for-granted assumptions (see **formal theory**).

Interpretivist approach One of three social theories about the nature of society (see **consensus theory** and **conflict theory**). In contrast to structuralist views, this view adopts an interpretivist or subjective view about the nature of society and seeks to understand the social world by looking more at the interactions between social groups and individuals – it seeks to understand and analyse how individuals construct and interpret their social lives. Principally, the subjective perspective looks to 'meaning' as the central feature which requires analysis, in other words – 'what does this action/behaviour mean to this individual?' and 'what are the ways meanings are constructed and interpreted?' The interpretivist approach supports a **therapeutic-helping approach** to understanding the purpose of social work and reveals a **social constructionism** approach to practice, helping the service user better understand their difficulties.

Issue-based approach to learning (IBL) A variant of problem-based learning (PBL). An IBL is an approach to learning and teaching that aims to promote **deep-rooted or meaningful learning**, alongside a concern to develop a critically reflective and analytic practitioner. Such an approach encourages us to think about the ideas that inform our practice so that we become aware of the relationship or link between theory and practice and therefore we are in a better position to critique our standpoint and those of others. Learners engage in learning activities (such as case studies and reflective exercises) that are relevant and engaging, allowing them to make sense and understand new learning.

Leadership and management Here the centrality of the person responsible, that is the leader, and their professional qualities are recognised rather than just a focus on the tasks required, i.e. management. It is about the role of effective leadership and valuing the workforce and developing their potential. This view supports a **human relations management** approach to understanding management and is concerned with the qualities required to create and support practices aimed at improving service provision and design and encouraging greater participation and involvement of people who use services. The quality of leadership is therefore seen as a crucial aspect of management.

Learning organisations Defined by the Social Care Institute for Excellence as an organisation that contains the following characteristics: an organisational structure that supports service user and carer participation; integrated team working and collaboration across the organisation and with other agencies; a strong organisational culture that supports learning of the workforce and utilisation of research and evidence to improve practice; effective and meaningful information systems that are understood and used across the organisation; commitment towards workforce development and support; and finally, leadership that is responsive to change across the whole organisation.

Maintenance approach One of three conceptualisations about the role or purpose of social work (Dominelli, 2002) which supports a **consensus** view about the nature of society. This approach reflects a view about social work that reinforces a need for compliance to the dominant *status quo* and where social work is viewed largely as a pragmatic activity. Change is sought at an individual level; difficulties either have practical solutions, as in the provision of a service, or individuals are encouraged and supported to deal more effectively with their situation, or are expected to reform in some way, for instance, in work with offenders. The emphasis is on a 'better fit' between the individual and the social environment, helping them with their difficulties so that they are able to manage more effectively and in line with socially expected behaviours. This approach does not seek social change but sees social work as contributing towards the maintenance of the dominant social system. Payne (2005) describes this approach as representing an individualist–reformist view about the purpose of social work.

Managerialism A term adopted from the business sector and applied to public services that seek to increase efficiency, effectiveness and economy in service provision. Managerialism emphasises the role of the manager as a key driver in reforming services and increasing their efficiency. Its roots lie in the individual rights and responsibilities discourse and the application of market principles in the provision of welfare. This can result in practice that becomes highly regulated, characterised by rigid procedures and a commitment to outcome measures (see **modernisation**).

Modernisation Reflects an overall emphasis on service regulation in order to raise standards, drawing on a number of factors; performance indicators and league tables; an emphasis on 'best-value' and effective practice models; partnership working and co-ordination between different welfare professionals and their organisations; increasing service user participation; greater public accountability and; registration and discipline of social care workers and continuous professional development.

Proactive approach to practice Based on supporting individuals and groups in gaining greater control over their lives and a greater sense of social participation in local environments. Part of an **empowerment** approach to practice.

Reflection A generic term used to describe the cognitive process involved in thinking about an incident or experience, using the skills of critical enquiry and interrogation, in order to make better sense of the experience and thereby enhance our understanding and improve our learning and practice.

Reflective practitioner Used to describe a practitioner who is prepared to interrogate their practice, by thinking critically about their actions and the ideas that guide their practice. It describes the process of attempting to improve practice through the process of **reflection**.

Reflexive–therapeutic view (see **therapeutic–helping approach**).

Social action theory (see **interpretivist approach**).

Socialist–collectivist view (see **emancipatory approach**).

Social constructionism An approach that emphasises different constructions or meanings about a phenomenon, in our case, social work. These different constructions about 'what social work is' arise from the influence of different and important factors, such as context, time, legislation and people's behaviour. These factors influence the judgements we make. Social constructionism implies that social relations and activities are not universally 'set' or predetermined, but are open to interpretation and negotiation. The construction of 'what we know' is a product of human meaning-making and not objective, fixed facts.

Social exclusion A concept used to describe multiple deprivation resulting from a lack of personal and social as well as political and financial opportunities. As a means of understanding multi-dimensional disadvantage, the concept allows for the acknowledgement that social exclusion is a phenomenon that can cut across all social groups and result in increased social and psychological instability for anyone.

Social theories These are theories drawn from the social sciences, especially the discipline of sociology, and provide explanations about the nature of society.

Strengths perspective Supports an empowering approach to social work practice since it seeks to focus on the service user's strengths or potential, rather than a preoccupation with their difficulties or problems (see **empowerment**). It is part of a value position about the nature of social work as well as part of a practice methodology. It attempts to work in partnership with service users and carers, supporting them in identifying their protective factors, or sources of resilience, and seeks to develop these as empowering strategies that can promote positive outcomes for the service user.

Structuralist approach (*see* **conflict theory** and **consensus theory**).

Subjective (*see* **interpretivist approach**).

Supervision Provides a vital role in supporting and managing practice for all the workforce across the organisation. In addition, it provides an educative function and should be a supportive process.

Theory Represents a set of related ideas and assumptions that are drawn upon to help explain something. Theory acts as an explanatory framework that attempts to help make sense of a phenomenon. Theories help structure and organise our thinking and are central to helping us make sense of our practice and what we do (see **formal theory** and **informal theory**).

Therapeutic-helping approach One of three conceptualisations about the role or purpose of social work (Dominelli, 2002) which supports an **interpretivist** view about the nature of society. This view about the nature or purpose of social work focuses on individual change and psychological functioning as the basis for intervention. The relationship between worker and service user is an important and intimate one, where personal insight is encouraged in order to help the service user function or manage their difficulties more effectively (*see* Payne (2005) who describes this approach as representing a reflexive–therapeutic view).

Utilitarianism–consequentialism One of three ethical theories which underpin beliefs about how social workers ought to behave. This approach draws upon the principle that the morality or rightness of an action is determined by whether its outcome is favourable or unfavourable. In social work, given the importance of multiple accountabilities, Banks (2006) suggests that two important principles inform this approach. First, the principle of utility which is concerned to promote 'the greatest good for the greatest number', and second, the principle of justice, which is concerned with distributing services as widely and/or fairly as possible (*see* **deontological** and **virtue ethics**).

Values Representative of general preferences and shaping our beliefs and attitudes. They tend to describe 'what is good and desirable' or worthwhile (Loewenberg and Dolgoff, 1992). They influence our behaviour and have an affective quality as well; that is, they impact on our emotions (*see* **ethics**).

Virtue or **character-based ethics** One of three ethical theories which underpin beliefs about how social workers ought to behave. This approach emphasises the integrity of the worker, or their motives, rather than focusing on the morality of the outcome or concentrating on a sense of duty and the person's behaviour. Virtue ethics are less concerned with questions about 'what is good social work?' and instead concentrate more on the qualities or character of the person and thus emphasise 'what is a good social worker?' (*see* **deontological** and **utilitarianism–consequentialism**).

References

Adams, R (2002) Social work processes. In Adams, R, Dominelli, L and Payne, M (eds) *Social work: Themes, issues and critical debates*. 2nd edition. Basingstoke: Palgrave/Open University Press.

Adams, R (2003) *Social work and empowerment*. 3rd edition. Basingstoke: Palgrave.

Audit Commission and Social Services Directorate (2004) *Old virtues, new virtues*. London: Audit Commission.

Banks, S (2006) *Ethics and values in social work*. 3rd edition. Basingstoke: Palgrave.

Barry, M and Hallett, C (eds) (1998) *Social exclusion and social work*. Lyme Regis: Russell House.

Beckett, C and Maynard, A (2005) *Values and ethics in social work: An introduction.* Sage: London.

Beresford, P (2000) Service users' knowledges and social work theory: conflict or collaboration, *British Journal of Social Work*, 30 (4), 489–503.

Bilson, A and Ross, A (1999) *Social work management and practice: Systems principles*. 2nd edition. London: Jessica Kingsley.

Bolton, G (2005) *Reflective practice: writing and professional development*. 2nd edition. London: Sage.

Bolzan, N and Heycox, K (1998) Use of an issue-based approach in social work education. In Boud, D and Feletti, G (eds) *The challenge of problem based learning*. 2nd edition. London: Kogan Page.

Boud, D, Cohen, R and Walker, D (1993) *Using experience for learning*. Buckingham: Open University Press.

Bowles, W, Collingridge, M, Curry, S and Valentine, B (2006*) Ethical practice in social work.* Buckingham: Open University Press.

Brechin, A (2000) Introducing critical practice. In Brechin, A, Brown, H and Eby, M (eds) *Critical practice in health and social care*. London: Sage/Open University.

British Association of Social Workers (2002) *The code of ethics for social workers*. Birmingham: BASW.

Brookfield, S (1987) *Developing critical thinkers*. Milton Keynes: Open University Press.

Brown, K and Rutter, L (2006) *Critical thinking for social work*. Exeter: Learning Matters.

Burden, T and Hamm, T (2000) Responding to socially excluded groups. In Percy-Smith, J (ed.) *Policy responses to social exclusion: towards inclusion?* Buckingham: Open University Press.

Cassuto Rothman, J (1998) *From the front lines: Students' cases in social work ethics*. Boston, MA: Allyn & Bacon.

Clark, C (2006) Moral character in social work, *British Journal of Social Work,* 36 (1), 75–89.

Coulshed, V and Mullender, A with Jones, D and Thompson, N (2006) *Management in social work*. 3rd edition. Basingstoke: Macmillan.

Cowger, C, Anderson, K and Snively, C (2006) Assessing strengths: The political context of individual, family and community empowerment. In Saleebey, D (ed.) *The strengths perspective*. 4th edition. Boston, MA: Allyn & Bacon.

Crawford, K and Walker, J (2007) *Social work and human development*. 2nd edition. Exeter: Learning Matters.

Cree, V (2002) Social work and society. In Davies, M (ed.) *Companion to social work*. 2nd edition. Oxford: Blackwell.

Croft, S and Beresford, P (1993) *Citizen involvement: A practical guide for change*. Basingstoke: Macmillan.

Croft, S and Beresford, P (2002) Service users' perspectives. In Davies, M (ed.) *Companion to social work*. 2nd edition. Oxford: Blackwell.

Department of Health (1998) *Modernising social services: Promoting independence, improving protection, raising standards* (Cmd 4169). London: Stationery Office.

Department of Health (2006) *Careers in social work*. 2nd edition. London: Stationery Office.

Dominelli, L (2002) Anti-oppressive practice in context. In Adams, R, Dominelli, L and Payne, M (eds) *Social work: Themes, issues and critical debates*. 2nd edition. Basingstoke: Palgrave/Open University Press.

DuBois, B and Miley, K (1999) *Social work: An empowering profession*. 3rd edition. Boston, MA: Allyn & Bacon.

Fook, J (2002) *Social work: Critical theory and practice*. London: Sage.

Ford, P, Johnson, B, Mitchell, R and Myles, F (2004) Social work education and criticality: Some thoughts from research, *Social Work Education*, 23 (2), 185–98.

Ford, P, Johnson, B, Mitchell, R and Myles, F (2005) Practice learning and the development of students as critical practitioners: Some finds from research, *Social Work Education*, 24 (40), 391–407.

General Social Care Council (GSCC) (2002) *Codes of practice for social care workers and employers*. London: GSCC.

Gibbons, J and Gray, M (2002) An integrated and experience-based approach to social work education: The Newcastle model, *Social Work Education*, 21 (5), 529–49.

Gould, N (1996) Introduction: Social work education and the 'crisis of the professions'. In Gould, N and Taylor, I (eds) *Reflective learning for social work, research, theory and practice*. Aldershot: Arena.

Hafford-Letchfield, T (2006) *Management and organisations in social work*. Exeter: Learning Matters.

Hanson, M (1995) Practice in organisations. In Meyer, C and Mattaini, M (eds) *The foundations of social work practice*. Washington, DC: NASW Press.

Healy, K (2000) *Social work practices: Contemporary perspectives on change*. London: Sage.

Healy, K (2005) *Social work theories in context: Creating frameworks for practice*. Basingstoke: Palgrave.

Howe, D (1987) *An introduction to social work theory*. Aldershot: Arena.

Howe, D (2002) Relating theory to practice. In Davies, M (ed.) *Companion to social work*. 2nd edition. Oxford: Blackwell.

Hudson, B (2005) New Labour and the public sector: A tale of two green papers, *Journal of Integrated Care*, 13 (4), 6–11.

International Federation of Social Workers (IFSW) (2001) Definition of social work, *Ethics in social work: statement of principles*. IFSW.

Johns, R (2007) *Using the law in social work*. 3rd edition. Exeter: Learning Matters.

Jones, C (2001) Voices from the front line: state social workers and New Labour, *British Journal of Social Work*, 31 (4), 547–62.

Jones, C (2002) Social work and society. In Adams, R, Dominelli, L and Payne, M (eds) *Social work themes: Issues and critical debates*. 2nd edition. Basingstoke: Palgrave/Open University Press.

Jones, R, Jimmieson, N, and Griffiths, A (2005) The impact of organisational culture and reshaping capabilities on change implementation success: The mediating role of readiness for change, *Journal of Management Studies*, 42 (2), 361–86.

Jordan, B (2000) Conclusion: Tough love: social work practice in UK society. In Stepney, P and Ford D (eds) *Social work models, methods and theories: A framework for practice*. Lyme Regis: Russell House.

Jordan, B (2001) Tough love: Social work, social exclusion and the third way, *British Journal of Social Work*, 31 (4), 527–46.

Knott, C and Scragg, T (eds) (2007) *Reflective practice in social work*. Exeter: Learning Matters.

Kuit, J, Reay, G and Freeman, R (2001) Experiences of reflective teaching, *Active Learning in Higher Education*, 2 (2), 128–42.

Light, G and Cox, R (2001) *Learning and teaching in higher education*. London: Sage.

Loewenberg, F and Dolgoff, R (1992) *Ethical decisions for social work practice*. 4th edition. Itasca, IL: F.E. Peacock.

Lymbery, M (2007) Social work in its organisational context. In Lymbery, M and Postle, K (eds) *Social work: A companion to learning*. London: Sage.

McBeath, G and Webb, S (2002) Virtue ethics and social work: Being lucky, realistic and not doing one's duty, *British Journal of Social Work*, 32 (8), 1015–36.

Meyer, C and Palleja, J (1995) Social work practice with individuals. In Meyer, C and Mattaini, M (eds) *The foundations of social work practice*. Washington, DC: NAWS.

Mills, S (1997) *Discourse*. Abingdon: Routledge.

Moon, J (1999) *Reflection in learning and professional development*. Abingdon: Routledge.

Mullender, A and Perrott, S (2002) Social work and organisations. In Adams, R, Dominelli, L and Payne, M (eds) *Social work themes: Issues and critical debates*. 2nd edition. Basingstoke: Palgrave/Open University Press.

Oko, J (2006) Evaluating alternative approaches to social work: A critical review of the strengths perspective, *Families in Society*, 87 (4), 601–11.

Oko, J and Jackson, M (2007) Human growth and development. In Adams, R (ed.) *Foundations of Health and Social Care*. Basingstoke: Palgrave.

Orme, J (2000) Social work: the appliance of social science – a cautionary tale, *Social Work Education*, 19 (4), 323–34.

Orme, J (2002) Feminist social work. In Adams, R, Dominelli, L and Payne, M (eds) *Social work themes: Issues and critical debates*. 2nd edition. Basingstoke: Palgrave/Open University Press.

Osmond, J and O'Connor, I (2004) Formalizing the unformalized: Practitioners' communication of knowledge in practice, *British Journal of Social Work,* 34 (5) 677–92.

Parker, J and Bradley, G (2007) *Social work practice: Assessment, planning, intervention and review*. 2nd edition. Exeter: Learning Matters.

Parker, J and Randall, P (1997) *Using theories in social work*. Birmingham: BASW/OLF.

Parrot, L (2006) *Values and ethics in social work practice*. Exeter: Learning Matters.

Parton, N (1996) An introduction. In Parton, N (ed.) *Social theory, social change and social work*. Abingdon: Routledge.

Parton, N (2002) Postmodern and constructionist approaches to social work. In Adams, R, Dominelli, L and Payne, M (eds) *Social work themes: Issues and critical debates.* 2nd edition. Basingstoke: Palgrave/Open University Press.

Parton, N and O'Byrne, P (eds) (2000) *Constructive social work: Towards a new practice*. Basingstoke: Macmillan.

Payne, M (1997) *Modern social work theory*. 2nd edition. Basingstoke: Macmillan.

Payne, M (2002) Management. In Adams, R, Dominelli, L and Payne, M (eds) *Critical practice in social work*. Basingstoke: Palgrave.

Payne, M (2005) *Modern social work theory*. 3rd edition. Basingstoke: Palgrave.

Pierson, J and Thomas, M (2002) *Dictionary of social work*. 2nd edition. Glasgow: HarperCollins.

Powell, M (2003) The third way. In Alcock, P, Erskine, A and May, M (eds) *The student's companion to social policy*. 2nd edition. Oxford: Blackwell.

Pugh, D (1993) Understanding and managing organizational change. In Mabey, C and Mayon-White, B (eds) *Managing Change*. 2nd edition. London: Paul Chapman Publishing.

Sakamoto, I and Pinter, R (2005) Use of critical consciousness in anti-oppressive practice: Disentangling power dynamics at personal and structural levels, *British Journal of Social Work*, 35 (4), 435–52.

Saleebey, D (2006) *The strengths perspective in social work practice*. 4th edition. Boston, MA: Allyn & Bacon.

Skills for Care (2006) *Leadership and management: A strategy for the social care workforce*. Available from www.topssengland.co.uk

Social Care Institute for Excellence (2004) *Characteristics of a social care learning organisation*. Available from www.scie.org.uk

Social Care Institute for Excellence (2004) *Has service user participation made a difference to social care services? Position Paper 3*. Available from www.scie.org.uk

Stepney, P (2000a) An overview of the wider policy context. In Stepney, P and Ford, D (eds) *Social work models, methods and theories: A framework for practice.* Lyme Regis: Russell House.

Stepney, P (2000b) Implications for social work in the new millennium. In Stepney, P and Ford, D (eds) *Social work models, methods and theories: A framework for practice.* Lyme Regis: Russell House.

Stepney, P (2000c) The theory to practice debate revisited. In Stepney, P and Ford, D (eds) *Social work models, methods and theories: A framework for practice.* Lyme Regis: Russell House.

Swindell, M and Watson, J (2007) Ethical delegates in the social work classroom: A creative pedagogical approach, *Journal of Social Work Values and Ethics,* 4, (1).

Thompson, N (2000) *Theory and practice in human services*. 2nd edition. Buckingham: Open University Press.

Thompson, N (2005) *Understanding social work: Preparing for practice*. 2nd edition. Basingstoke: Palgrave.

Thompson, N (2006) *Anti-discriminatory practice*. 4th edition. Basingstoke: Palgrave.

Trevithick, P (2005) *Social work skills: A practice handbook*. 2nd edition. Berkshire: Open University Press.

Williams, F (1998) Agency and structure revisited: Rethinking poverty and social exclusion. In Barry, M and Hallet, C (eds) *Social exclusion and social work*. Lyme Regis: Russell House.

Wilson, A and Beresford, P (2000) Anti-oppressive practice – emancipation or appropriation?, *British Journal of Social Work*, 30 (5), 553–73.

Wilson, G (1998) Staff and users in the post-modern organisation: Modernity, post-modernity and users' marginalisation. In Barry, M and Hallet, C (eds) *Social exclusion and social work*. Lyjme Regis: Russell House.

Index

Added to the page references, 'f' denotes a figure and 'g' denotes the glossary.

Transforming Social Work Practice – titles in the series

To order, please contact our distributor: BEBC Distribution, Albion Close, Parkstone, Poole, BH12 3LL. Telephone: 0845 230 9000, email: **learningmatters@bebc.co.uk**. You can also find more information on each of these titles and our other learning resources at www.learningmatters.co.uk.